This book is dedicated to the memory of my dear father Jack Collins.

RADIOS
THE · GOLDEN · AGE

PHILIP COLLINS

CHRONICLE BOOKS · SAN FRANCISCO

Printed by Dai Nippon Printing Co., Hong Kong.

Library of Congress Cataloging in Publication Data
available.

Editing: Charles Robbins
Book and cover design: Arnold Schwartzman

Distributed in Canada by
Raincoast Books
112 East 3rd Avenue
Vancouver, B.C.
V5T 1C8

10 9 8 7 6 5 4 3 2 1

Chronicle Books
San Francisco, CA

CONTENTS:

"I belong to the radio of the month club."

INTRODUCTION:

Over the last twenty years, we have succumbed to the disposable. Throwaway pens, lighters, razors, and polystyrene cups are all part of life in the fast lane. Cheap synthetic compounds have made disposables possible, and we have embraced them utterly.

Today's lifestyles are directed to the easy way, and plastic is valued by consumers for its expedience. Of course, there was a time when plastic created a tremendous revolution in both design and mass production. And now we are oddly nostalgic for those earlier years and the wonderful products they brought us.

Table radios were among the first goods to be made of plastic. Chicago Molded Products built the first plastic cabinet in 1931 for Kadette. Phenolic, Urea, Casein, and other plastic compounds accounted for 95 percent of table models by 1950, and wood had become the staple of TV sets and console radios, although early televisions had occasionally been housed in plastic. Metal and mirrored radio cabinets were made in very limited numbers.

Many of the six hundred manufacturers flourishing in the United States between the late twenties and early forties sought to put a "radio in every room." They hired famous industrial designers to contribute to inherent obsolescence by introducing new models every year. Raymond Loewy, Russel Wright, Serge Chermayeff, and Dorwin Teague were all recruited to foster imaginative variations in cabinet style.

Radio programs themselves remained the same, but the staggering variety of designs from those years is evidence of a golden era when creativity, ingenuity, and productivity gave us exciting radio cabinets. In designing them, the artist hoped to reflect the streamlined and moderne concepts, ideas usually associated with automobile radiator grilles, railroad engines, and airplanes.

Today, the miniaturization of parts has eroded our desire for innovative cabinet design. Instead, boxes in brushed aluminum offer blinking lights and touch-sensitive buttons for the stereo enthusiast. Radios can now be a plastic box the size of a cigarette pack or a large "ghetto blaster" trailing a deafened mass of unwilling listeners in its wake.

The old radios photographed here suggest that there was indeed life before Rock and Roll, and it came through four inch speakers. Radio was the most important source of news and entertainment in the first half of this century.

Sadly, most of the receivers that gave us the nightly reports of Hitler's activities in Europe, of the explosive demise of the airship Hindenburg, of Joe Louis' defeat of Max Schmeling, and of Orson Welles' production of "The War of the Worlds," are now resting under layers of dust in attics and cellars. Many have, however, been rescued. The following pages record some memories of an age when the table radio could not only be listened to but also admired.

Daily---1,800,000
Sunday-3,150,000

NEWS

NEW YORK'S PICTURE NEWSPAPER

FINAL

FAKE RADIO 'WAR' STIRS TERROR THROUGH U.S.

Story on Page 2

"War" Victim

"I Didn't Know".

In an attempt to propagate the idea of a radio for every room, manufacturers keenly pursued the opportunity to produce frivolous designs as merchandising tie-ins with films, sports figures, radio programs, or consumer products.

The famous Charlie McCarthy set features a molded metal effigy of our hero, perched on a ledge in front of the speaker grille and gazing benignly at the listener. Hopalong Cassidy, Snow White, Mickey Mouse, The Lone Ranger (unfortunately without Tonto), and the Dionne Quintuplets all promoted five-tube sets bearing their popular images.

Corporations were keen to get their messages across, not only through their sponsored shows but additionally in visual representation of their product; hence the Coke bottle radio, the Coca-Cola Cooler and Pepsi refrigerator radios, the various beer and champagne bottle radios, the Champion Sparkplug radio, and the radio station radio (in the shape of a large microphone with the appropriate station initials emblazoned above.)

The nicotine fancier was treated to the Smokerette with a provision for four pipes, loose tobacco, cigarettes, and ashtray, all molded into a brown bakelite design which incidentally housed a radio. Baseball fans were not ignored. The "Mickey Mantle" reminded the listener who hit the most homers.

Tipplers had to wait until 1945 before they could enjoy the Porto Baradio, featuring decanters and glasses and recesses for entertaining at cocktail hour. Movie stars and others with money were indulged with expensive mirrored sets that reflected not only the buyers' lovely faces but also the blue and peach interiors of their Hollywood mansions. A "Mother's Day" set was offered at $35 in 1947 for affluent children to express their appreciation of Mom.

Imaginative designers cloaked Amplitude Modulation sound in a variety of disguises — cameras, dice, book cases, clocks, skyscrapers, ships, globes, bottles, pianos, and jewelry cases. Here then, for all those who don't know a megacycle from a ten speed, are those extraordinary radios of yesteryear. The music goes around and around, and it comes out here

12 ILLUSTRATIONS

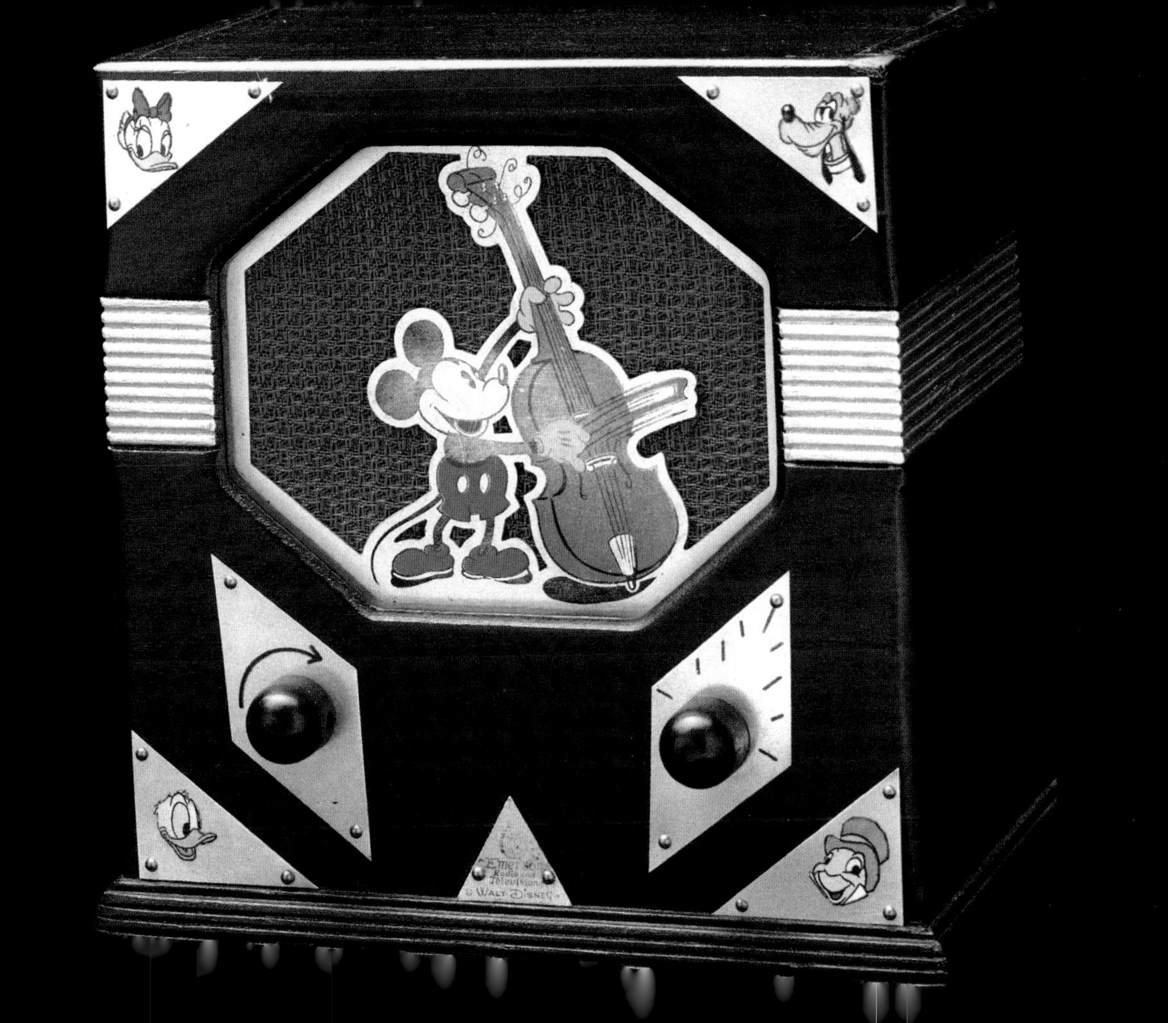
Radio
WALT DISNEY

The Ultimate in Design...

THREE SUPERB COLOR COMBINATIONS

Black and Gold, and Maroon and Gold at $59.50—Old Ivory and Gold at $62.50. Complete with Radiotrons. Prices slightly higher on West Coast.

5-tube AC-DC Dual-Wave Superheterodyne receiver with 7-tube performance in power and natural tone. 3-gang condenser, automatic volume control, double-grille dynamic speaker base—all of unusually substantial, shock-proof construction. Height, 16 inches. Globe and base design covered by U. S. Patent. Licensed under patents of Radio Corporation of America. Fully guaranteed by the Colonial Radio Corporation.

COLONIAL RADIO CORPORATION, BUFFALO, N. Y.

The Selling Sensation!

Colonial presents the

A brilliant, all-surpassing achievement of designing and engineering genius . . . giving the recognized highest quality radio a magnificent modern revolving world globe setting in heavy moulded bakelite and actual gold-plated metals.

Nothing in radio has ever created such an overwhelming sensation . . . or won such an immediate response from the trade and the public as has the NEW WORLD Radio by Colonial. Here is a merchandising "NATURAL"—a selling FORCE which stops the crowds and SELLS—which is, above all, the perfect radio in construction and performance.

Be the first in your city to feature this new leader. Our literature, newspaper mats, publicity and other sales promotion will help you to get the utmost from this outstanding opportunity.

Distributed by Graybar

Distributed exclusively by the 73 Branch Houses of the Graybar Electric Co., Inc. Ask your nearest branch for discounts and terms—or write direct to Graybar Electric Co., Inc., Graybar Bldg., New York, N.Y. *Get Demonstration Models NOW. Make Early Reservations for Shipments.*

COLONIAL RADIO CORPORATION, BUFFALO, N. Y.

Colonial "New World" 1933

1 2 3 4 5 6 7 8 9 10

Unknown 1934

18 Emerson 1935

AIR KING

A NEW TYPE OF RADIO...
...INTRODUCED IN A NEW WAY

Kadette Distributors Rendering Unique Service to Dealers

Right Now—this month Kadette jobbers are sending to 10,000 dealers samples of the new Kadette Jewel radio. Also an illustrated announcement of the entire International Kadette Line. This is new in radio merchandising. There is no "High Pressure" salesmanship here. You are permitted to look over the 1935 Kadette, taking your own time.

Let Kadette Speak for Itself

When you open your Demonstration Package don't stop at admiring its amazing beauty. Put the Kadette Jewel to every reception test you can think of and you will marvel at its performance. Take it apart and see the simplest, cleanest, most rugged chassis ever designed. You'll then know why Kadette alone can offer their famous "One year-one dollar" service guarantee.

Complete Merchandising and Dealer Help Service

Don't fail to study the merchandising plan for retailers. Take advantage of the dealer helps that come with Kadette assortments—window and counter displays, circulars for mail or personal distribution and newspaper ad and mat service. Put into operation the merchandising suggestions evolved by one of radio's outstanding merchandising authorities.

• • •

The Kadette Line is up to the minute—alive. Priced from $13.50 to $34.50 to meet the demand. Don't overlook the many outstanding values in larger models. Note especially the prices of the 1935 Kadette Line. Here is a proposition that is "out of the rut". Get in on a good thing. Order your assortments and start selling NOW.

DEALERS—If you have not received your Kadette Jewel sample or received notice of its shipment, get in touch immediately with your jobber. In territories not now served by Kadette Jobbers, the factory will upon request mail you your demonstration package at full discount, C. O. D., transportation prepaid.

JOBBERS—Over fifty leading jobbers are co-operating in introducing by mail this new exceptional radio. There is still some territory open. If you want a product with a sales plan that will quickly boost your sales at a lower sales cost—Wire today.

KADETTE Jewel

LIST PRICE $13.50

International Radio Corp. Ann Arbor, Mich.

Kadette "Jewel" 1935

PAUL WHITEMAN solves a mystery
and gives a clue to finer radio music
1 ON THE DANCE FLOOR
OH, MR. WHITEMAN, HOW DIFFERENT YOUR MUSIC SOUNDS —IT WAVERS SO ON MY RADIO
STRANGE— IT MUST BE YOUR RADIO
2
HOW WOULD YOU TWO LIKE TO SEE INSIDE A RADIO STUDIO? I'M GOING OVER IN A FEW MINUTES
OH, HOW THRILLING— I'VE ALWAYS WANTED TO SEE THEM BROADCAST
3 IN RADIO CITY
THESE ARE THE BIG RCA TUBES ALL THE LARGE STATIONS DEPEND ON
AND, OF COURSE, OUR ENGINEERS CHANGE THEM REGULARLY TO INSURE THE VERY CLEAREST TONE
4
AHA—MAYBE THAT'S WHAT YOUR SET NEEDS —NEW TUBES
THAT'S THE ONE THING WE FORGOT. THEY'RE ABOUT A YEAR OLD, I'LL HAVE THEM TESTED FIRST THING
5 A WEEK LATER
OH, MR. WHITEMAN, YOUR MUSIC COMES IN FINE ON OUR RADIO NOW. WE HAVE A NEW SET OF MICRO-SENSITIVE RCA RADIO TUBES
THAT'S GREAT— TELL YOUR FRIENDS ABOUT IT. THEY WANT BETTER RECEPTION, TOO
NEW LIFE FOR OLD RADIOS!
Quicker start! More power! Better tone! It really means *new life* for your set when you replace old, worn radio tubes with these new Micro-Sensitive tubes by RCA. These are the only tubes *guaranteed* by RCA Radiotron Company to give you 5 important improvements in tube performance... Have your dealer test your tubes today and replace those that are worn. Insist on RCA Radio Tubes —and bring back the thrill of radio.
New Micro-Sensitive RCA Radio Tubes give you:
1 Quicker Start
2 Quieter Operation
3 Uniform Volume
4 Uniform Performance
5 Every Tube is Matched
MADE IN U.S.A.
2A5
RCA Cunningham Radiotron
RCA
RCA Cunningham Radiotron
RADIO TUBES

Coronado
RADIO
TUBE
R. C. A.
LICENSED
Gamble Stores

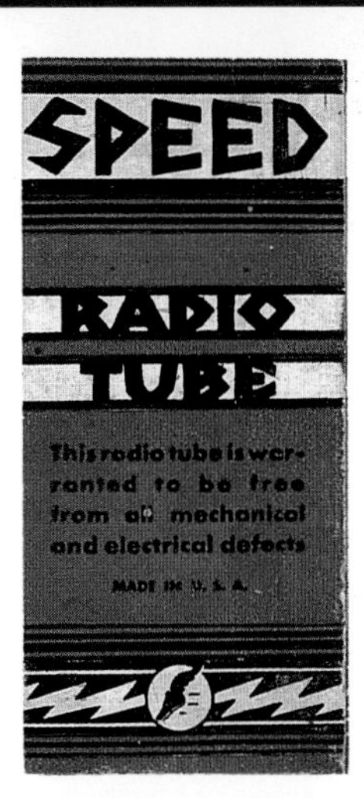
SPEED
RADIO
TUBE
This radio tube is warranted to be free from all mechanical and electrical defects
MADE IN U. S. A.

BOND
REG. U.S. PAT. OFF.
HIGH VACUUM
RADIO
TUBE
BOND ELECTRIC CORPORATION
JERSEY CITY, N.J.

ACE
RADIO
TUBE
ACE
OF THE AIR

COMMANDER
RADIO
TUBE
Licensed
Licensed under patents and applications of the General Electric Company, Westinghouse Electric and Manufacturing Company, Radio Corp. of America, and associated companies.
Long Life
Guaranteed

FULL
TONE
RADIO
TUBE
EVERY TUBE
GUARANTEED

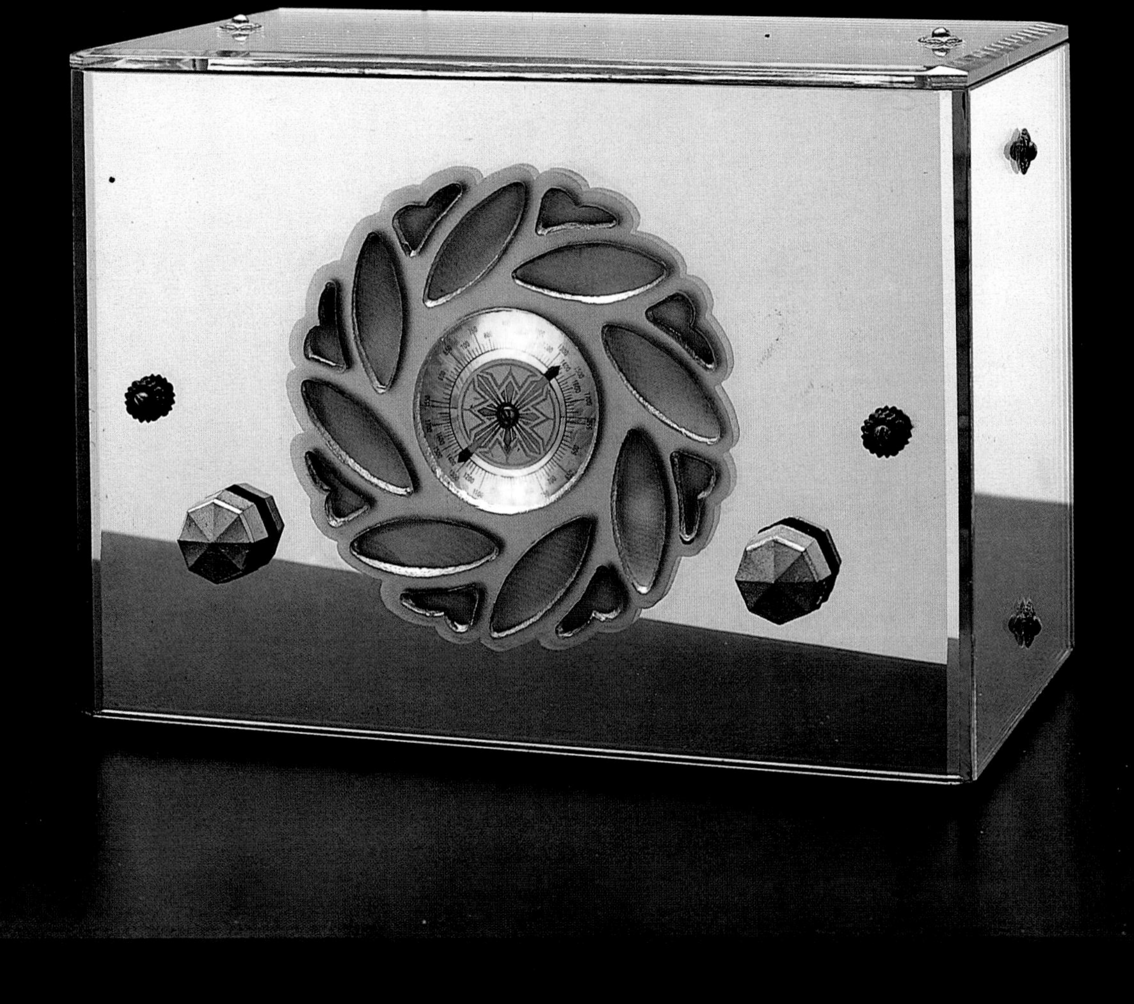

24 Unknown c. 1935

1200 1100 1000 900 800 750 700
KILOCYCLES
Sparton
1400 1500 1700 6 6.5 7
650 600 550 17 16 15 14
MEGACYCLES
7.5 8 9 10 11 12 13

NEW

COLORADIO SERIES

SERIES 254 FOR AC CURRENT

5 TUBE SUPERHETERODYNE FEATURING METAL TUBES AND BEAM POWER TUBE

The Most Powerful Small Set Made

CHASSIS FEATURES: 7 tube performance; Illuminated airplane dial calibrated in KC; Frequency range 535 to 1750 KC; Beam power output tube; Automatic overload control; Built-in antenna; I. F. Frequency 456 KC; Acoustically fitted dynamic speaker; Operates on 115 volts, 60 cycles, AC.

Model	Cabinet	Price
254W:	WALNUT BAKELITE CABINET	$22.95
254D:	BLACK BAKELITE WITH CHROMIUM	24.95
254V:	PURE IVORY CABINET	24.95
254R:	PURE CHINESE RED CABINET	24.95
254BG:	BLACK BAKELITE AND GOLD	24.95
254G:	IVORY AND GOLD	26.95
254RG:	CHINESE RED WITH GOLD	26.95

Prices include full tube equipment

MODEL 254T IN WALNUT WOOD CABINET WITH IDENTICAL CHASSIS FEATURES $24.95

FADA BATTERY COLORADIO

FOR THE FARM

SERIES 242 - 4 TUBE SUPERHETERODYNE OPERATES FROM 2 VOLT AIR CELL

CHASSIS FEATURES: 8 tube performance; 9 tuned circuits; Tunes American, Short Wave and Police Broadcasts; Frequency range 535-1750 KC and 2.2-6.9 MC; Illuminated airplane dial calibrated in KC and MC; Tone control; Phono-jack; Rubber mounted tuning condensers; 6 in. permanent magnet dynamic speaker; I. F. Frequency 456 KC; Automatic volume control; Air cell drain only .4 amps.

Model	Cabinet	Price
242W:	WALNUT BAKELITE CABINET	$31.50
242D:	BLACK BAKELITE AND CHROMIUM	36.50
242V:	PURE IVORY CABINET	36.50
242R:	PURE CHINESE RED CABINET	36.50
242BG:	BLACK BAKELITE AND GOLD	36.50
242RG:	CHINESE RED AND GOLD	41.50
242G:	IVORY AND GOLD	41.50

Prices include full tube equipment

SERIES 246 - 4 TUBE SUPERHETERODYNE OPERATES FROM 6 VOLT STORAGE BATTERY

CHASSIS FEATURES: Identical with Series 242 excepting special built-in "B" Eliminator and synchronous vibrator for power supply from 6 volt storage battery. Drain, only 1.45 amps.

Model	Cabinet	Price
246W:	WALNUT BAKELITE CABINET	$36.50
246D:	BLACK BAKELITE CABINET	41.50
246V:	PURE IVORY CABINET	41.50
246R:	PURE CHINESE RED CABINET	41.50
246BG:	BLACK BAKELITE AND GOLD	41.50
246RG:	CHINESE RED AND GOLD	46.50
246G:	IVORY AND GOLD	46.50

Prices include full tube equipment

Both Series obtainable in Walnut Wood Cabinets, Compact & Console Models.

FOR 12 PROFITABLE MONTHS IN 1937

FEATURED IN 7 DISTINCTIVE SERIES IN 8 MAGNIFICENT COLOR COMBINATIONS

and priced as low as **$19.99** *complete*

One of the oldest and surest devices used to command attention is the appeal of color. Color glorifies . . . Color is stimulating to the eye . . . Color creates the desire to buy. The appeal of color proves a strong selling ally because it is a "plus" feature. Color in radio is not new . . . but Coloradio by Fada is! Every Coloradio series possesses not only the appeal of color but also the new "Streamline" cabinet designs which blend with the majestic color combinations. No other small set line combines so many selling features to offer the consumer . . . Color . . . Streamline . . . Design . . . Performance . . . Value.

ATTRACTIVE COLORADIO DISPLAY NOW AVAILABLE

A new display designed for the new Fada Coloradio Series is available to all dealers.

SUEDE ZIPPER CARRYING CASES FOR ALL MODELS

Suede Zipper carrying bags for every Coloradio series are featured for as little as $2.50

FADA RADIO & ELECTRIC COMPANY

LONG ISLAND CITY, N. Y.

Fada 1937

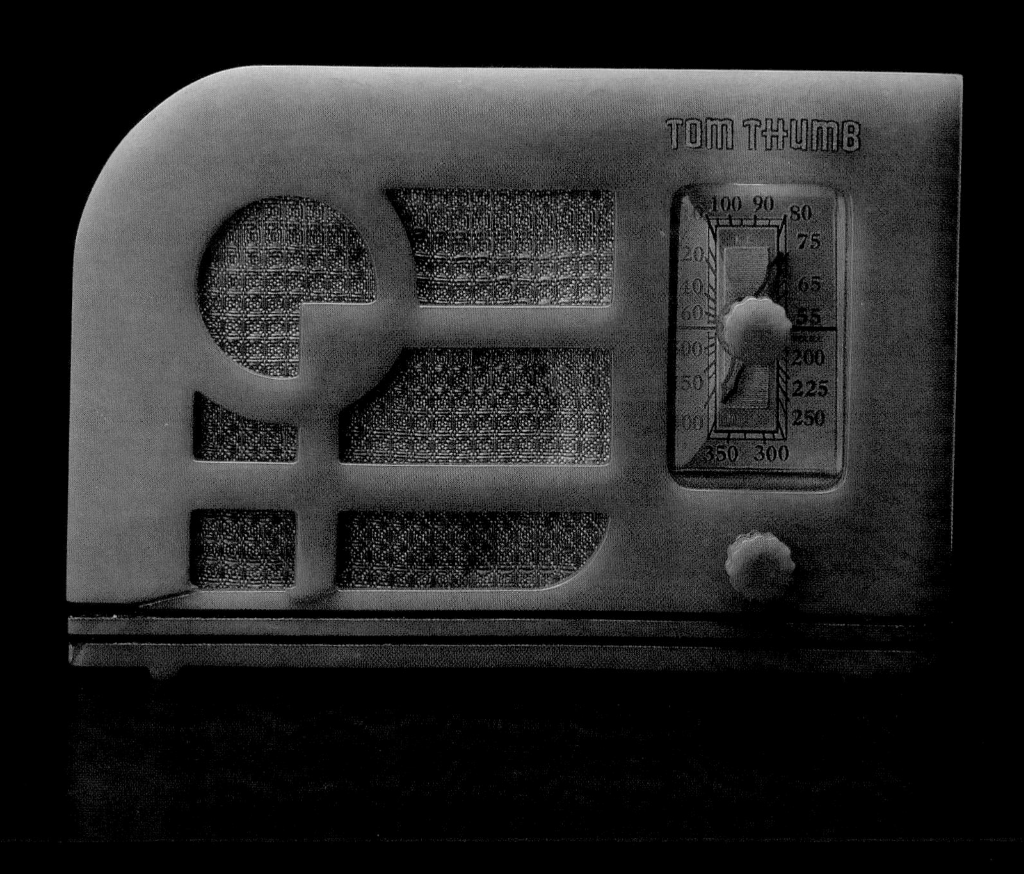

 Tom Thumb 1938

Emerson 1938

120
100
80
Emerson
Radio and
Television

90
110
70
130
KILOCYCLES
65
150
60
170
55
Emerson
Emerson

70 80 100 120
60
140
55
160
200
550
225
500
250 350 450
KILOCYCLES
METERS
FADA
Radio

32 Fada 1938

Detrola "Peewee" 1938

34 Airite 1938

Majestic "Charlie McCarthy" 1938

55
60
65
70
80

1200
1600
1300
1500
POLICE
1700
600
550

 Zenith 1938

120
140
160

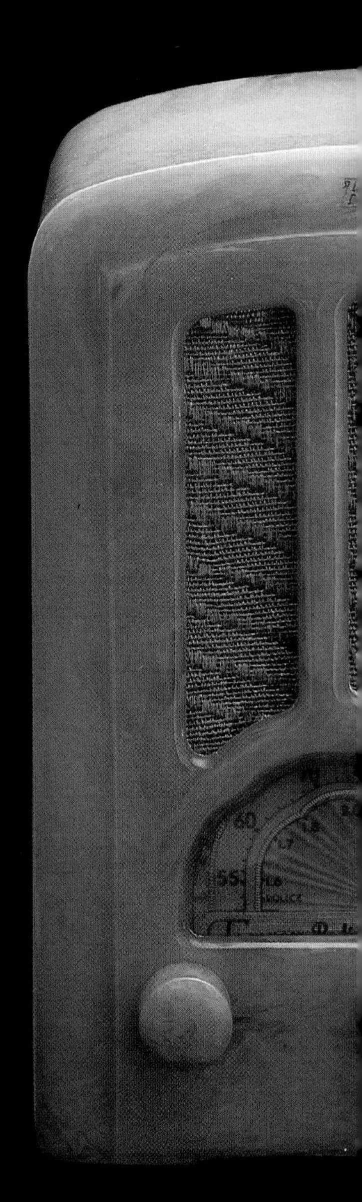

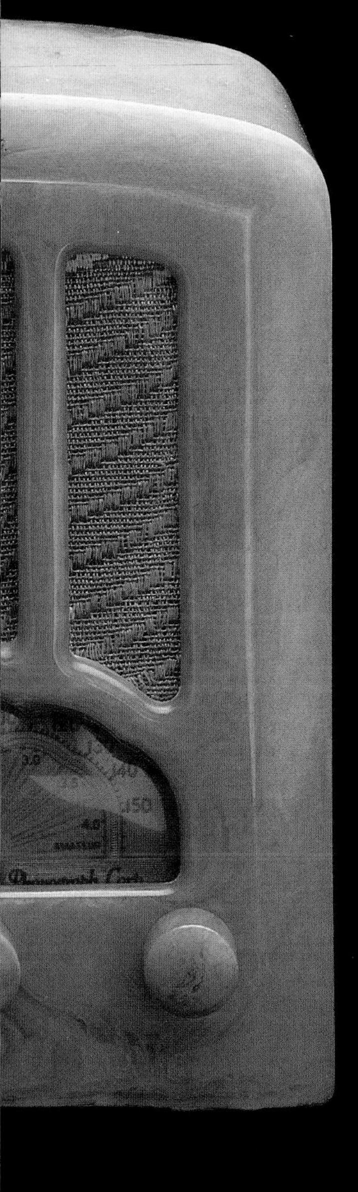

Emerson 1939 (left) and 1938 (center and right)

 Emerson 1939

General Electric 1939

FADA
Radio
SALES — SERVICE

FADA
Radio
AUTHORIZED DEALER

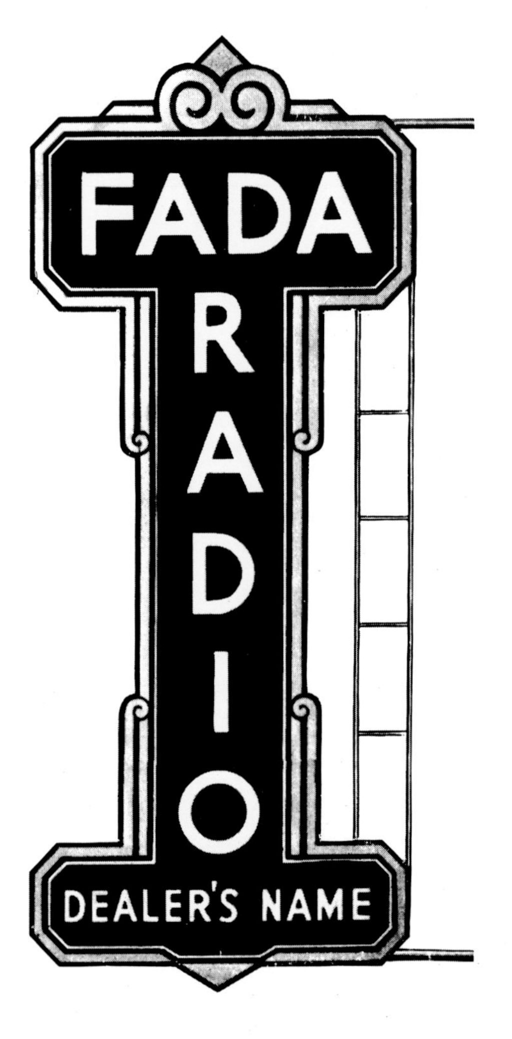
FADA
RADIO
DEALER'S NAME

FADA
Radio
with
AUTOMATIC
FLASHOGRAPH

130 100 80 70
150
170
550
500
60
55
175
200
400 300 250
METERS
FADA
Radio

Fada 1939

Sonora.1939

 Belmont 1940

Continental c. 1940

Addison

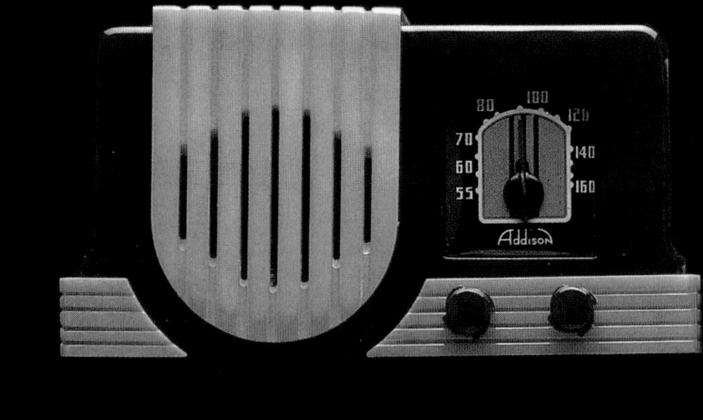
Addison

Addison

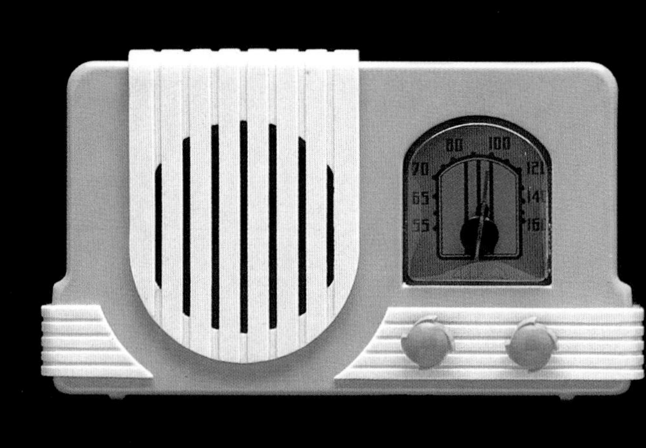

Addison

Addison

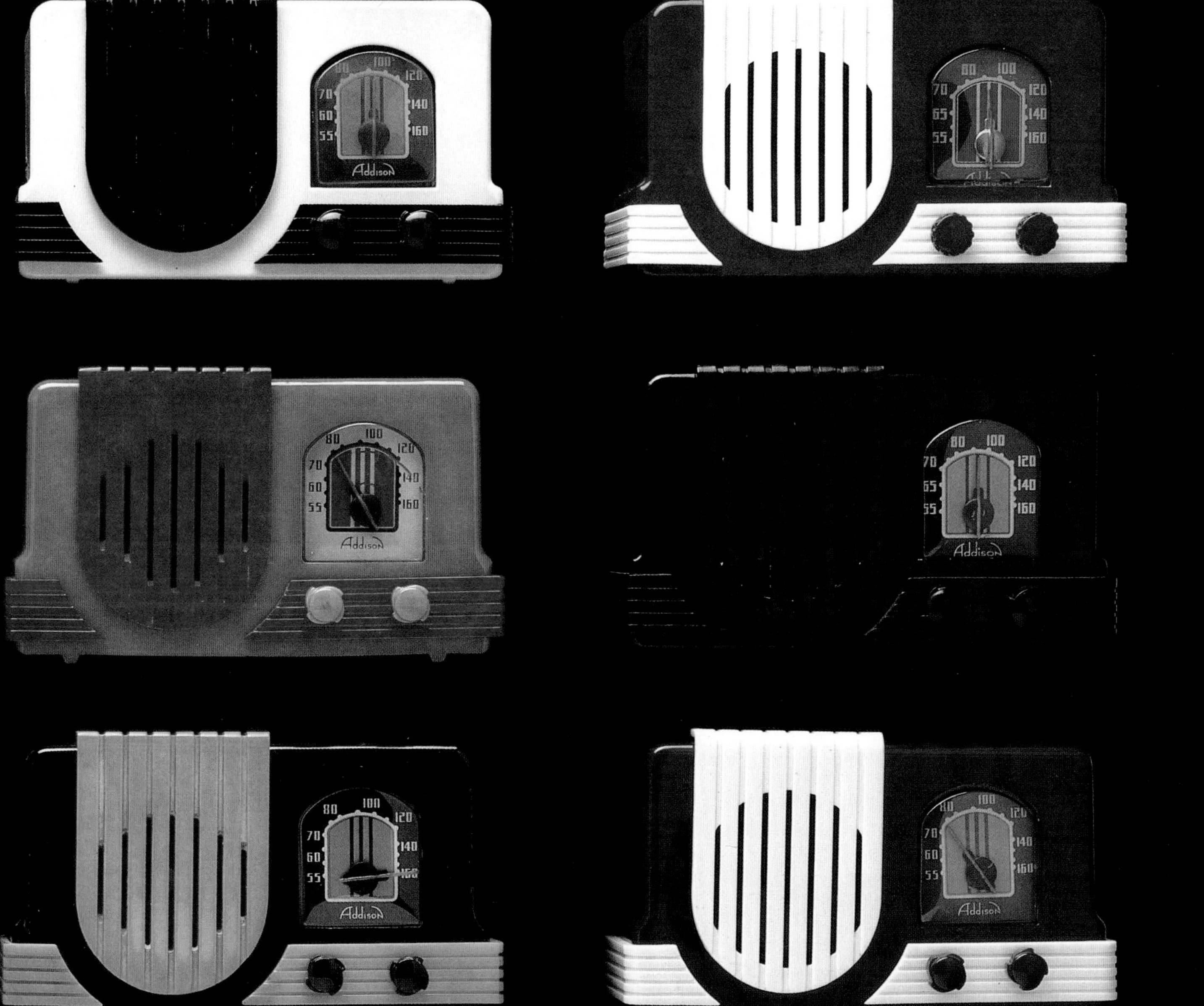
Addison
Addison
Addison
Addison
Addison
Addison

The "Patriot"

RED, WHITE and BLUE "All American" Scoop

by Emerson

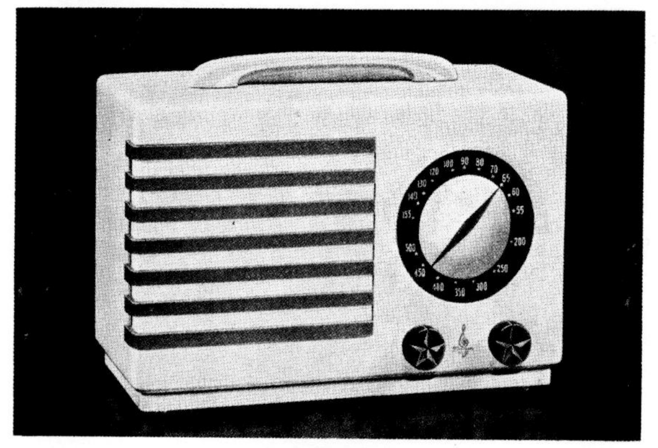

Model 400-2—Basic WHITE with Red and Blue
Model 400-3—Basic RED with White and Blue . . . Model 400-1—Basic BLUE with Red and White

$15

Slightly Higher in West and South

Never Before Such a Dramatic Radio Idea!

TIMELY! Electrifying! Crowd-Stopping! Red, White and Blue in 3 gorgeous color combinations! Display it in your window and store—use the powerful sales helps. Cash in on the nationwide publicity that will be given to "The PATRIOT" by Emerson!

Use the "Uncle Sam Hat" Display and Other Helps

Never Before Such a Great Radio Value . . . !

It's BIG — 11½ inches wide. It has a Built-In "Super-Loop" Antenna —2 Watts BEAM POWER Output—New Type Illuminated Dial—Large Dynamic Speaker—Monsanto Cabinet with Carrying Handle. Nothing ever like it at this SALES-MAKING price!

More Emerson PROFIT NEWS! Ask your Emerson Distributor for Broadside which tells "The PATRIOT" story and describes other sensational new Emerson models.

EMERSON RADIO & PHONOGRAPH CORP., NEW YORK, N. Y.
WORLD'S LARGEST MAKER OF HOME RADIO

Emerson Patriot (right) and Aristocrat (left) 1940

 Emerson 1940

Mitchel "Lumitone" 1940 (left) and Radiolamp Corp. of America c. 1940 (right)

6 6.5 7 8 10 12 14
55 60 70 80 100 120 140 160
BROADCAST

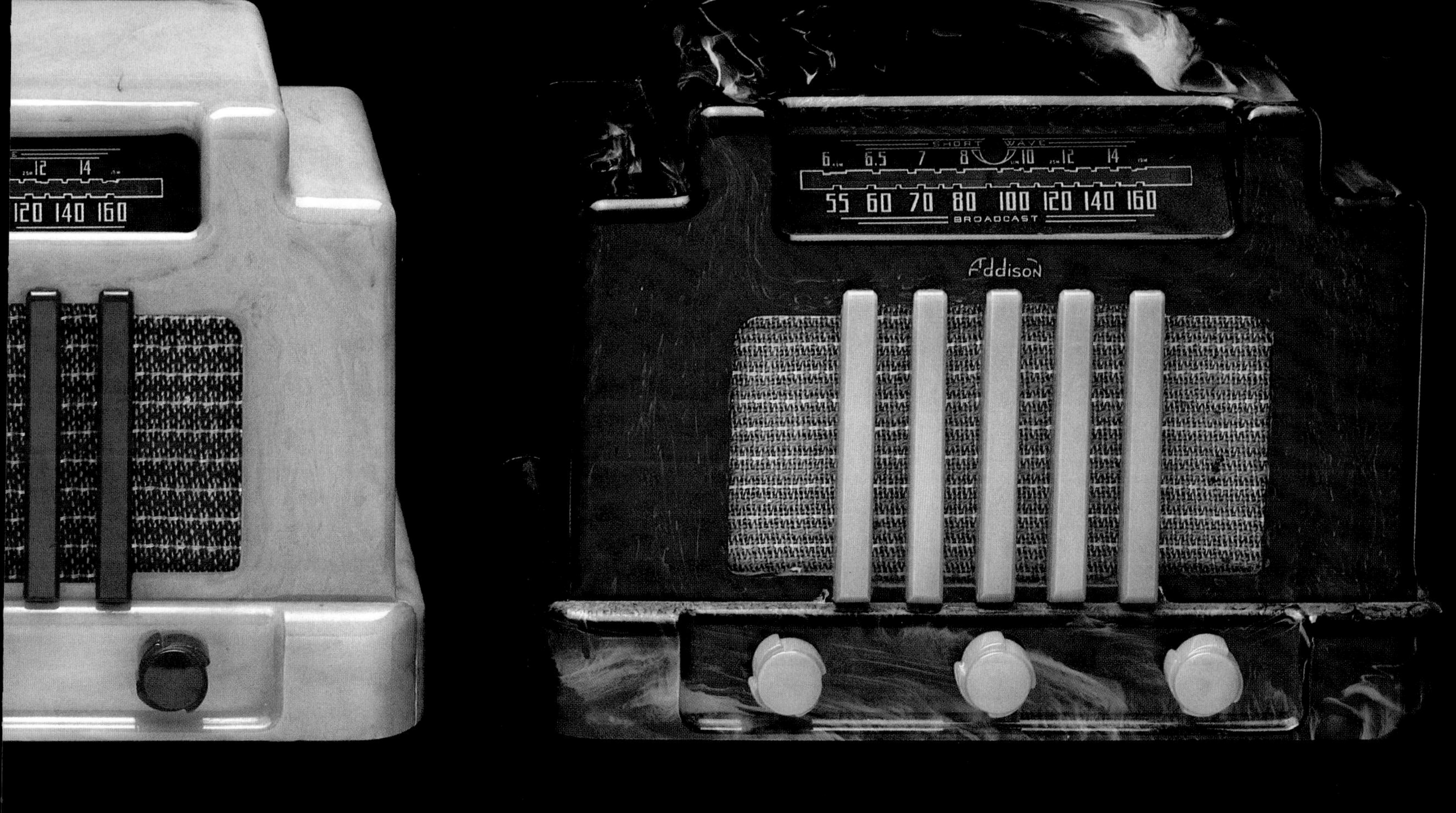

Addison c. 1940

 Garod "Commander" 1941

Trophy c. 1941

60 Sonora "Coronet" 1941

The New
CROSLEY
RADIOS
for 1936

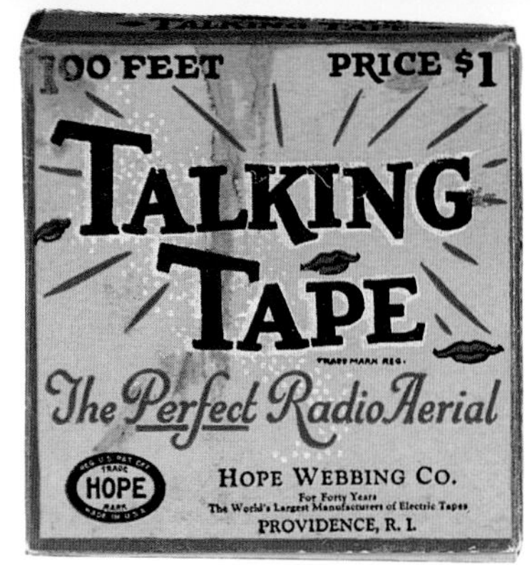
100 FEET
PRICE $1
TALKING TAPE
The Perfect Radio Aerial
HOPE
HOPE WEBBING CO.
For Forty Years
The World's Largest Manufacturers of Electric Tapes
PROVIDENCE, R. I.

DICK TRACY
AND THE
TIGER LILLY
GANG

Radio
PATROL
EDDIE SULLIVAN
CHARLIE SCHMIDT
THE BETTER LITTLE BOOK
CALLING
W-1-X-Y-Z
Jimmy Kean
and the
RADIO-SPIES
THE BETTER LITTLE BOOK
SAMPSON
STIKTAPE AERIAL
INSTANTLY INSTALLED
"The EAR
OF THE AIR"

 General Electric 1941

Westinghouse “Little Jewel” 1945

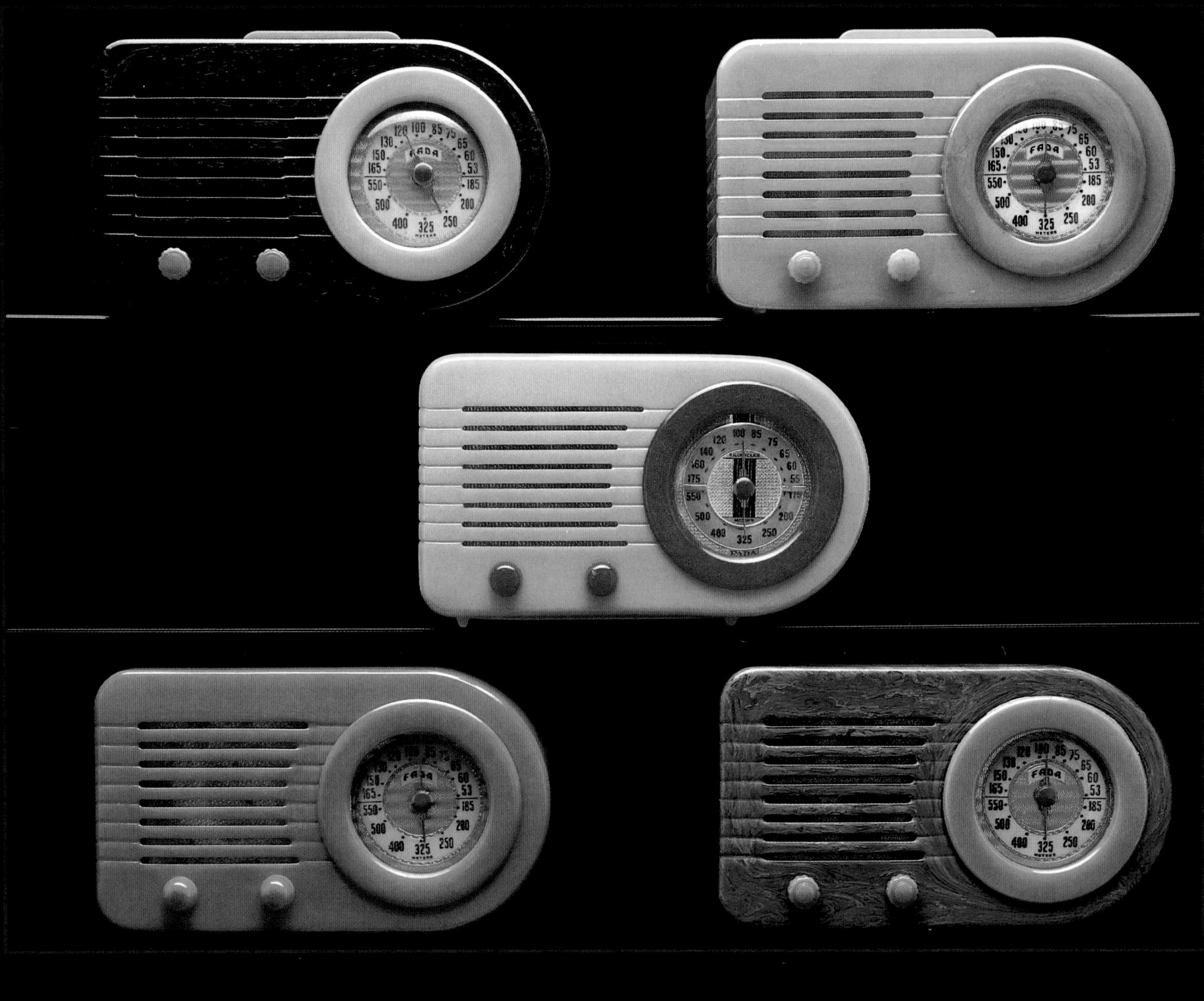

 Fada "Streamliner" 1946 and 1941 (center)

Fada "Streamliner" 1941

FADA
The
RADIO
of
TO-MORROW
TO-DAY!
TOPS
• IN BEAUTY
• IN DURABILITY
1000 SERIES
6 TUBES
Yes . . . "Tops" is the word for FADA. The FADA line of radios, brilliantly designed for beauty of appearance and precision made for beauty of tone, emphasizes the accuracy of our slogan, "The Radio of Tomorrow . . . Today."
And, back of the unmatched consumer acceptance of FADA's "radios of tomorrow" is the amazing durability of the FADA radio of yesterday. In every town and every city in the land there are FADA radios in everyday use . . . radios that have given ten, fifteen or twenty years of brilliant service.
Small wonder that these hundreds of thousands of satisfied users look forward to getting one of the new FADA receivers, equipped with Sensive-Tone for finer, clearer reception.
652 SERIES
6 TUBES
Small wonder that FADA good will, augmented year after year since broadcasting began, is your assurance of rapid, continuous sale of FADA radios for many years to come!
FADA
Sensive-Tone
FADA 6 tube models are equipped with the new FADA "Sensive-Tone" . . . assuring greater sensitivity and clearer reception.
PLACE YOUR FAITH IN
FADA
Radio
Famous Since Broadcasting Began!
FADA RADIO AND ELECTRIC COMPANY, INC., LONG ISLAND CITY, N. Y.

53 60 65 75 85 100 120 140 165
FADA
AMERICAN 54 60 65 75 85 100 120 140 165 BROADCAST
FOREIGN 6.0 6.5 7.0 8.0 FADA 12 14 16 18 SHORTWAVE
53 60 65 75 85 100 120 140 165
FADA
53 60 65 75 85 100 120 140 165
FADA

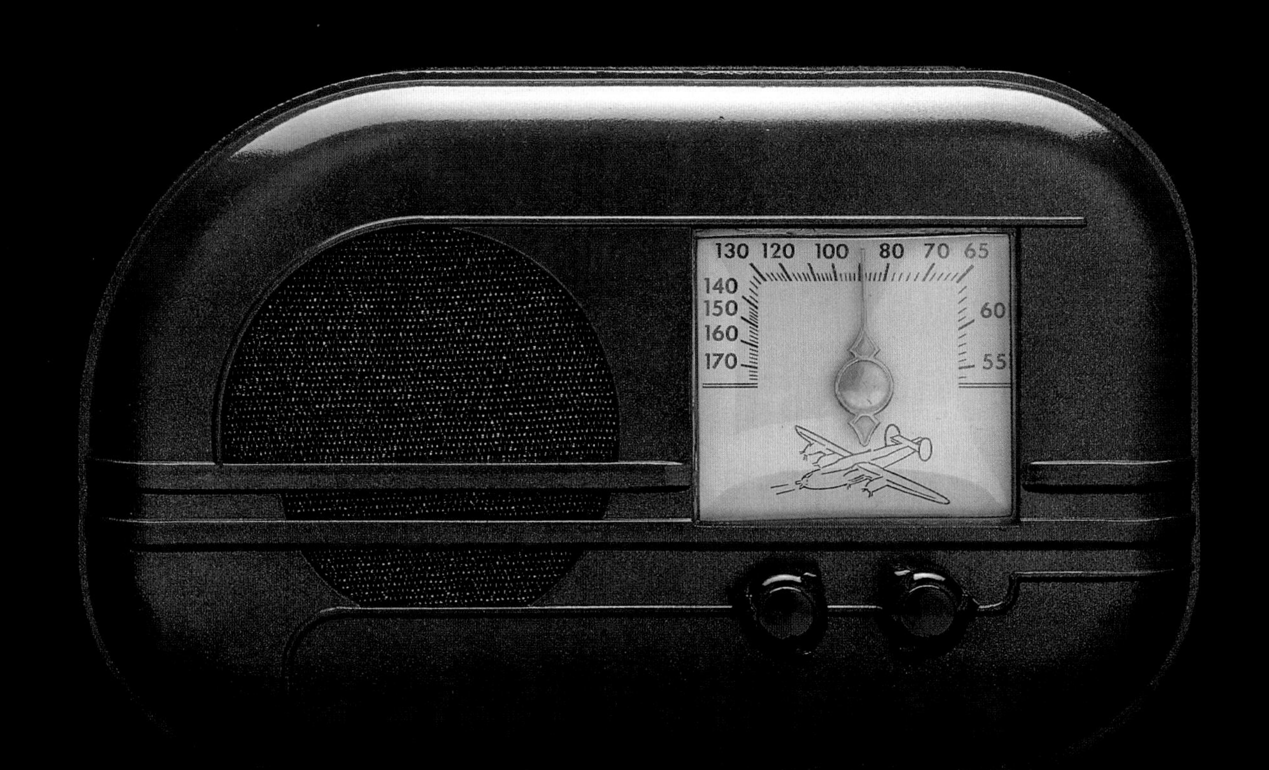

 Unknown c.1946

Belmont 1946

 Bendix 1946

Popular bakelite models 1938 to 1946

 Stewart Warner 1946

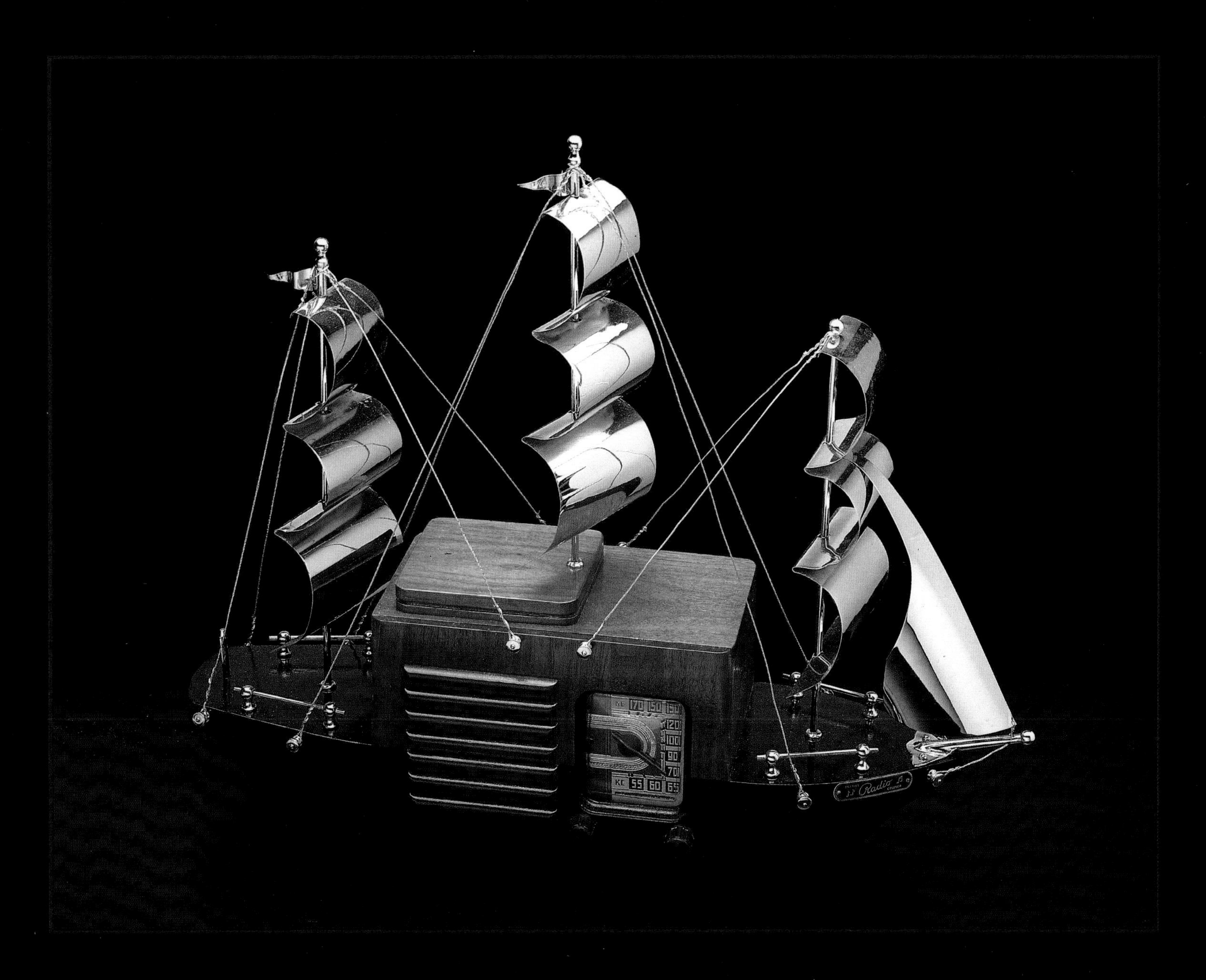

Majestic "Melody Cruiser" c. 1946

 DeWald 1946

Airline c. 1946

76 Crosley "Duette" 1946

Coronado 1947

 Stewart Warner "Air Pal" 1947

Sentinel
STANDARD BROADCAST
55 60 70 80 90 110 130 150 170
MADE IN U.S.A.

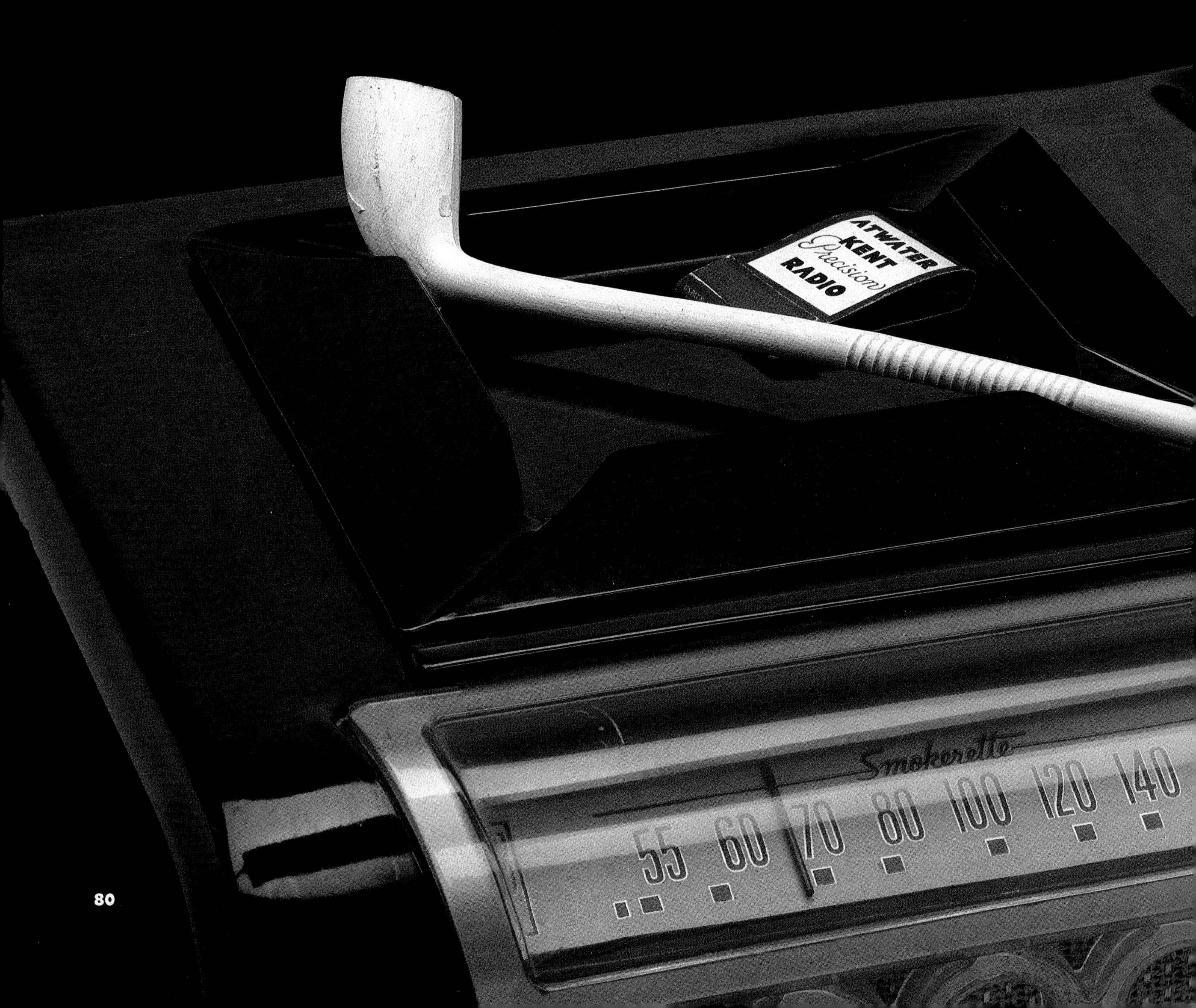
ATWATER
KENT
Precision
RADIO
Smokerette
55 60 70 80 100 120 140

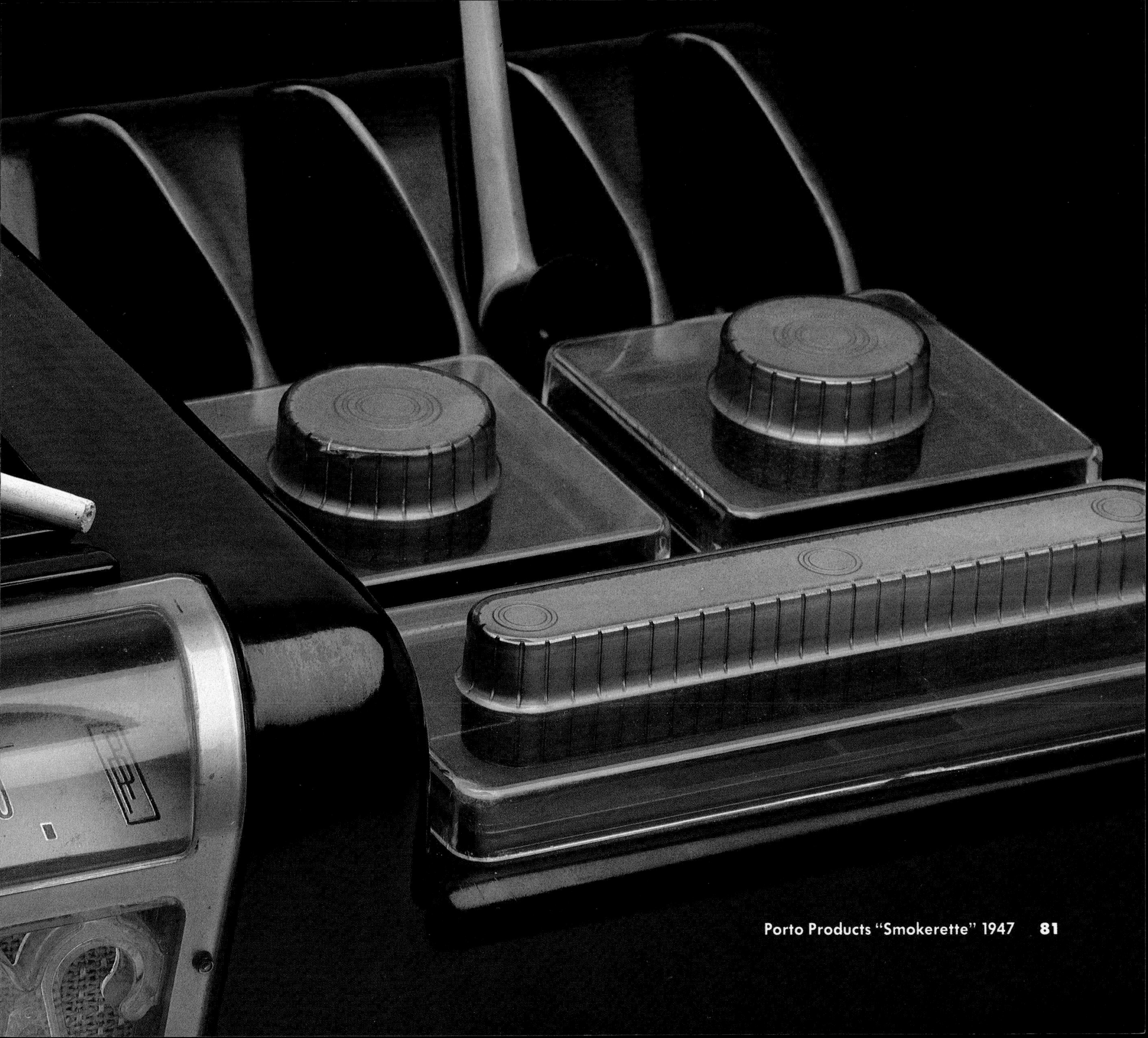

Porto Products “Smokerette” 1947

CROSSWORD PUZZLE

HORIZONTAL

1\. 5. Star in the portrait (CBS, Thursday nights)
8\. Felines
12\. Thomas ——, English composer (1710-78)
14\. Henry ——, singer
16\. Ire
17\. Meadow
19\. One of the Great Lakes
20\. Audibly
22\. A warning of danger
24\. Musical instrument
26\. Alan ——, announcer
27\. —— Stanley, bandleader
28\. A company of musicians
30\. Mountains in South America
33\. A hook for fastening
37\. Native inhabitant of New Zealand
38\. Cleanse lightly with clean water
39\. Dried plums
40\. Joe ——, comedian
41\. —— Fairchild, orchestra-leader
42\. Animal allied to the weasel
45\. —— Kent, radio actress
49\. Extinct bird of New Zealand
51\. Frances ——, radio actress
55\. —— Levy, radio actress
57\. Impart steadiness to
59\. Be ready for
60\. Worn over the top part of shoes
61\. Imperfect
63\. Time gone past
64\. Top hat (slang)
67\. Confederate
68\. Certain
69\. Lanny ——, tenor
70\. —— Johnson, radio actress

VERTICAL

2\. Masculine name
3\. Bob ——, announcer
4\. Feminine name
6\. To dive under water, as whales
7\. To rip
8\. Restrain
9\. Songs
10\. Virginia Clark plays "Helen ——"
11\. Crack, so as to let in water
13\. Spanish article
14\. To exist
15\. A crescent
18\. Facility
21\. Jack ——, singer
22\. Bow
23\. A matrix
25\. Werner ——, conductor
28\. Willow tree
29\. Land measure (pl.)
30\. Unit of electrical measurement
31\. Paul ——, announcer
32\. Feminine name
34\. Connection
35\. Publications issued yearly
36\. Weak cider
43\. Postpone temporarily
44\. Dashing effect
46\. Pertaining to law
47\. Country of Nino Martini's birth
48\. A lizard
49\. Substances fusible by heat
50\. Take in, as a sponge
52\. Male singing voice
53\. Large-toothed files
54\. A different one
56\. Chinese measure
58\. Initials of Arthur Peterson
61\. Feminine name
62\. Mexican tree
65\. Nose like that of a bulldog
66\. —— Maupin, orchestra-leader

 Crossword solution page: 119

Belmont 1947

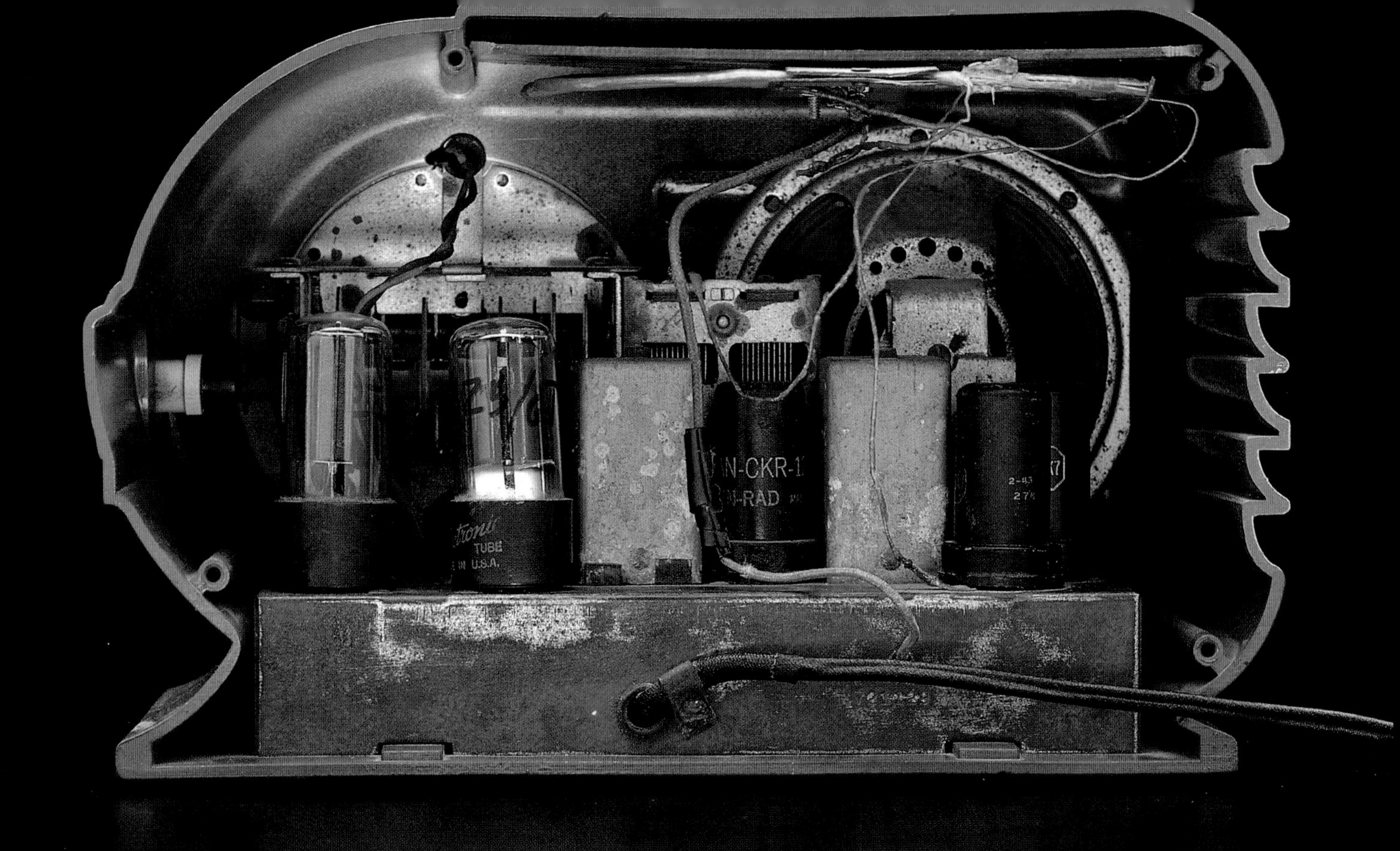
TUBE
IN U.S.A.
IN-CKR-1
N-RAD
2-43
27

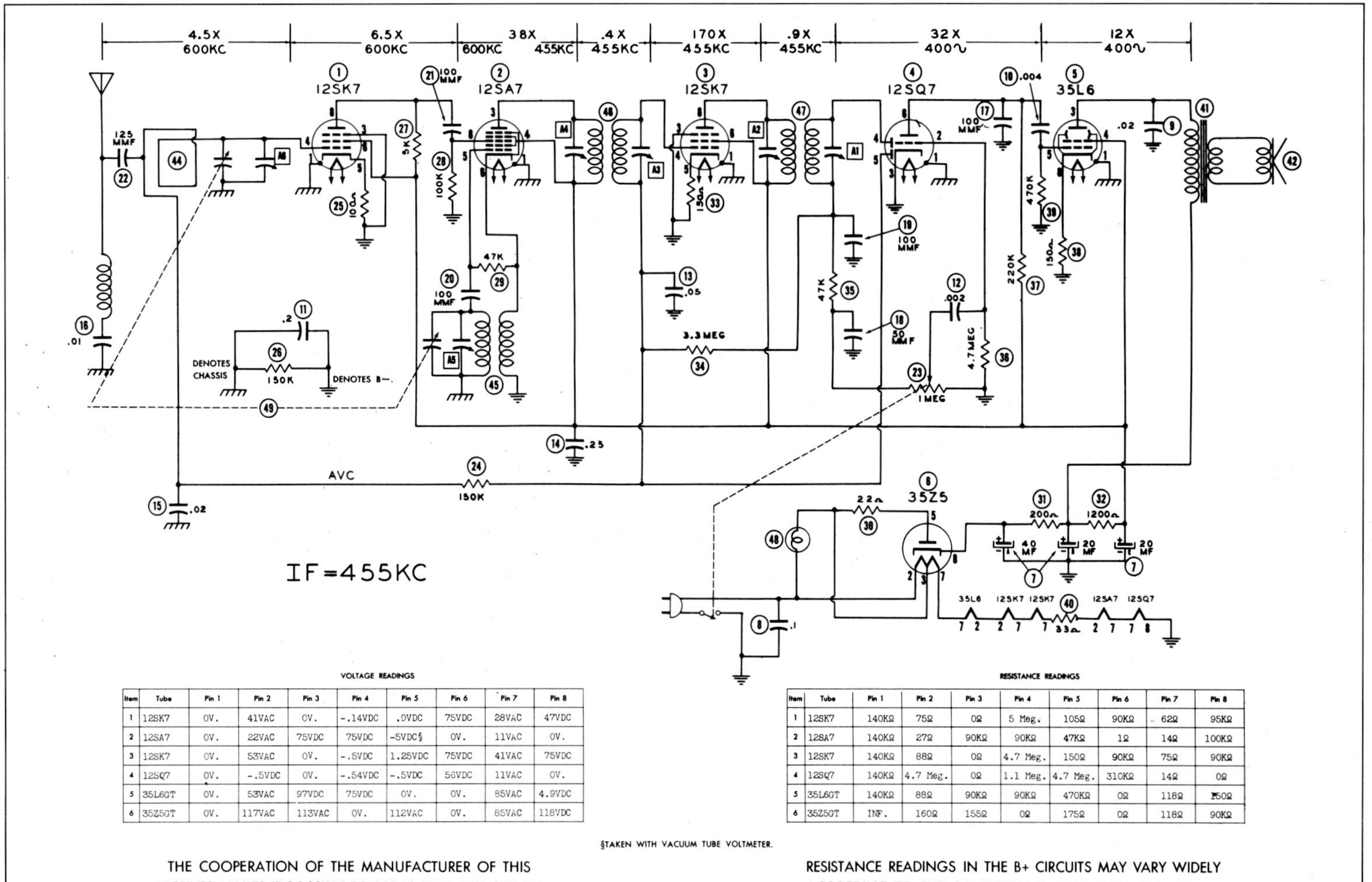

VOLTAGE READINGS

Item	Tube	Pin 1	Pin 2	Pin 3	Pin 4	Pin 5	Pin 6	Pin 7	Pin 8
1	12SK7	OV.	41VAC	OV.	-.14VDC	.9VDC	75VDC	28VAC	47VDC
2	12SA7	OV.	22VAC	75VDC	75VDC	-5VDC§	OV.	11VAC	OV.
3	12SK7	OV.	53VAC	OV.	-.5VDC	1.25VDC	75VDC	41VAC	75VDC
4	12SQ7	OV.	-.5VDC	OV.	-.54VDC	-.5VDC	56VDC	11VAC	OV.
5	35L6GT	OV.	53VAC	97VDC	75VDC	OV.	OV.	85VAC	4.9VDC
6	35Z5GT	OV.	117VAC	113VAC	OV.	112VAC	OV.	85VAC	118VDC

RESISTANCE READINGS

Item	Tube	Pin 1	Pin 2	Pin 3	Pin 4	Pin 5	Pin 6	Pin 7	Pin 8
1	12SK7	140KΩ	75Ω	0Ω	5 Meg.	105Ω	90KΩ	62Ω	95KΩ
2	12SA7	140KΩ	27Ω	90KΩ	90KΩ	47KΩ	1Ω	14Ω	100KΩ
3	12SK7	140KΩ	88Ω	0Ω	4.7 Meg.	150Ω	90KΩ	75Ω	90KΩ
4	12SQ7	140KΩ	4.7 Meg.	0Ω	1.1 Meg.	4.7 Meg.	310KΩ	14Ω	0Ω
5	35L6GT	140KΩ	88Ω	90KΩ	90KΩ	470KΩ	0Ω	118Ω	150Ω
6	35Z5GT	INF.	160Ω	155Ω	0Ω	175Ω	0Ω	118Ω	90KΩ

§TAKEN WITH VACUUM TUBE VOLTMETER.

THE COOPERATION OF THE MANUFACTURER OF THIS RECEIVER MAKES IT POSSIBLE TO BRING YOU THIS SERVICE

A PHOTOFACT STANDARD NOTATION SCHEMATIC

RESISTANCE READINGS IN THE B+ CIRCUITS MAY VARY WIDELY ACCORDING TO THE CONDITION OF THE FILTER CAPACITORS

4714-12

The stage gain measured values listed above are approximate values for an average operative stage, rather than an absolute value. It should be borne in mind that it is possible to introduce so many variables into the measurement operation, such as, type of equipment used for measuring, handling and placement of probes, the accuracy of alignment, etc., that an absolute reading is impractical. AVC is made inoperative and 3-volt battery bias substituted for measurement.

1. **DC Voltage measurements are at 20,000 ohms per volt; AC Voltages measured at 1,000 ohms per volt.**
2. **Socket connections are shown as bottom views.**
3. **Measured values are from socket pin to common negative.**
4. **Line voltage maintained at 117 volts for voltage readings.**
5. **Nominal tolerance on component values makes possible a variation of ± 10% in voltage and resistance readings.**
6. **Volume control at maximum, no signal applied for voltage measurements.**

55 60 70 80 90 110 130 150 170
DEWALD
K.C.
55 60 70

DeWald 1941 and 1948 (center)

YOUR HOST OF THE AIRWAVES

The Coca-Cola Company presents

EDGAR BERGEN with CHARLIE McCARTHY

CBS 8 p. m. EST every Sunday

And every day... wherever you travel, the familiar red cooler is your HOST OF THE HIGHWAYS... HOST TO THE WORKER in office and shop... HOST TO THIRSTY MAIN STREET the country over.

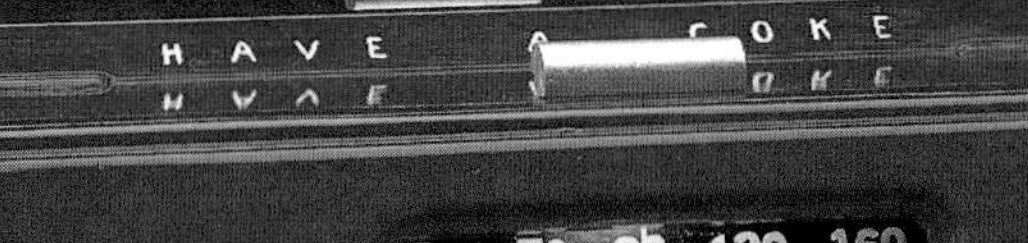
HAVE A COKE
55 70 90 120 160
60 80 100 140
DRINK
Coca-Cola
ICE COLD

HI PARDNER---
PROUD TO HAVE YOU JOIN UP

Quite a radio you have here. It's made specially for young cow pokes and cow gals who know something good when they see it. Now, let me tell you about it.

First thing, it'll play on either AC or DC power. It's not persnickety so long as the juice is between 105 and 115 volts. And it doesn't take a whole lot of juice either—only 30 watts (about half as much as an ordinary light bulb).

It's a mighty tough radio, too, with a solid steel case and a real rugged chassis. It can take real rough treatment if it has to—but then there isn't any point in treatin' it mean just because of that. Incidentally, it's Underwriters' Laboratories listed, too. That means it's been tested all kinds of ways and it's safe!

LISTED UNDER REEXAMINATION SERVICE UNDERWRITERS' LABORATORIES, INC. UL

NOW YOU'RE READY TO SADDLE UP

It doesn't make much difference where you set it, but it's best to keep it off the radiator or heater. Now, unwind the power cord and plug it in. If your bunk-house has AC current you can put the plug in either way and it will play. (Sometimes it will play better if you pull the plug out and turn it over and plug it back in. You can find out which way is best by trying both ways.) If you have DC current your radio will play with the plug pushed in just one way. So, if you're using DC and your radio doesn't work the first time you plug it in, pull out the plug and turn it over and plug it in the other way.

NOW UNCOIL THE LARIATENNA

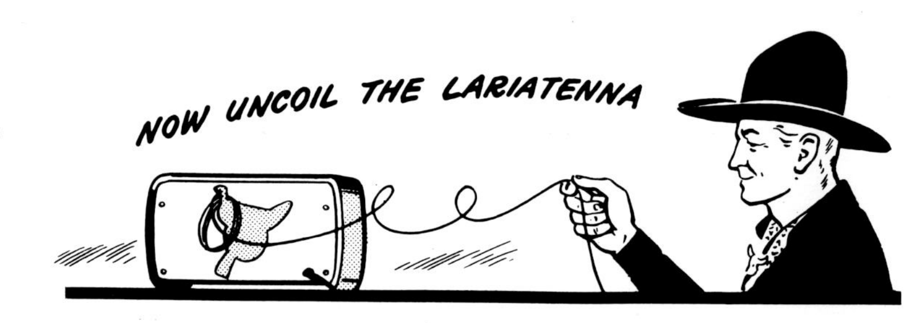

On the back of the radio, all coiled up and hung on the pommel of the saddle is your antenna. We call it the "Lariatenna" and if you use it like I tell you, you can rope in more stations than you can stuff in a ten gallon hat. Here's how.

- ★ **Take the Lariatenna off the saddle pommel.**
- ★ **Unwind it—clear out.**
- ★ **Stretch it out along the wall of the bunk-house. Not too tight.**
- ★ **Attach the suction cup to the window glass—or the bunk-house wall if Mom will let you.**
- ★ **That's all.**

Most places, you won't need all the 20 feet of the Lariatenna strung out. Maybe only a third of it or half of it. Coil what you don't need back on the saddle pommel.

When you string out the "Lariatenna," keep it close to the wall and out of the way. Keep it out of the middle of the bunk-house or you may get your spurs all tangled up in it and pull the radio off the table. And it will keep the women-folk happier if everything's neat. And, listen, Pardner, don't attach the "Lariatenna" to a water pipe, or radiator or the like. Those things are what they call "grounded" and this radio is designed to operate without ground connection.

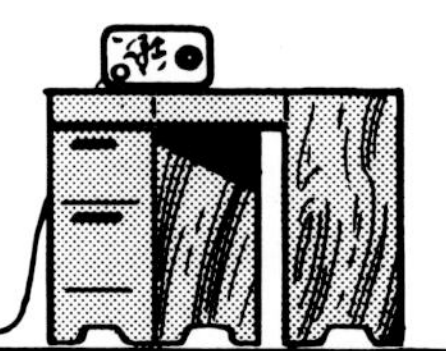

Arvin "Hopalong Cassidy" 1950

92 Unknown c. 1950

Arvin 1950

94 Arvin 1950

70 90 120 160
Majestic
60 80 100 140

 Silvertone 1951

CROSLEY
COLORADIOS
CROSLEY
55 60 70 80 100 120 140 160

98 Airline "Rudolph" 1951

LONE RANGER
Airline

Arvin

Arvin

ARVIN
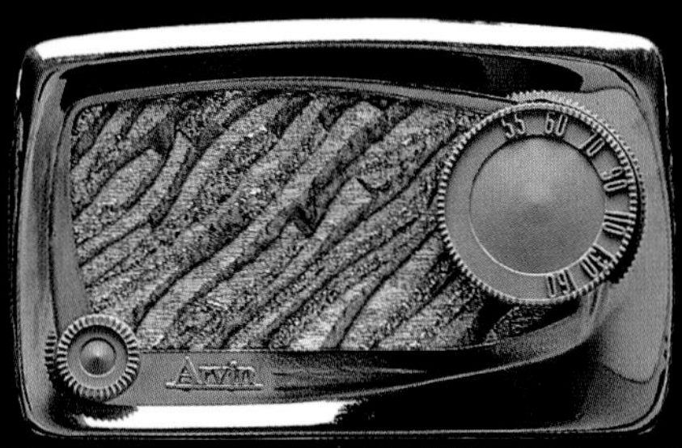
Arvin
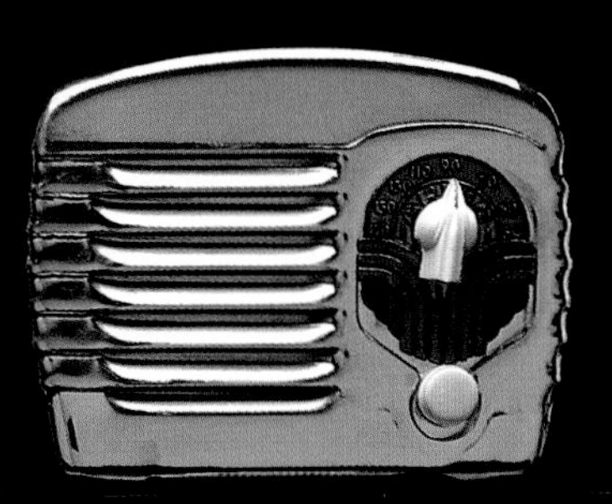

Arvin

Silvertone
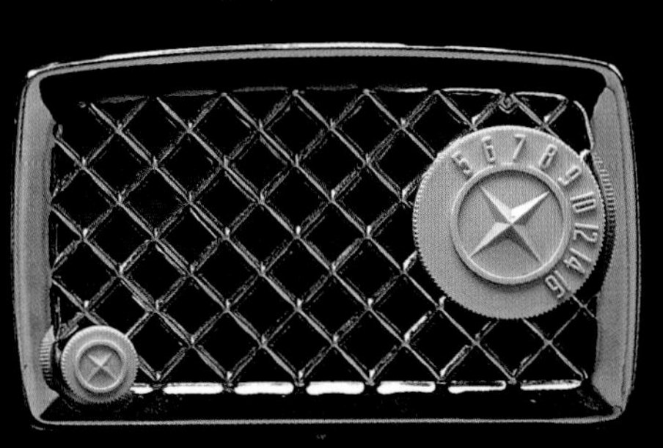

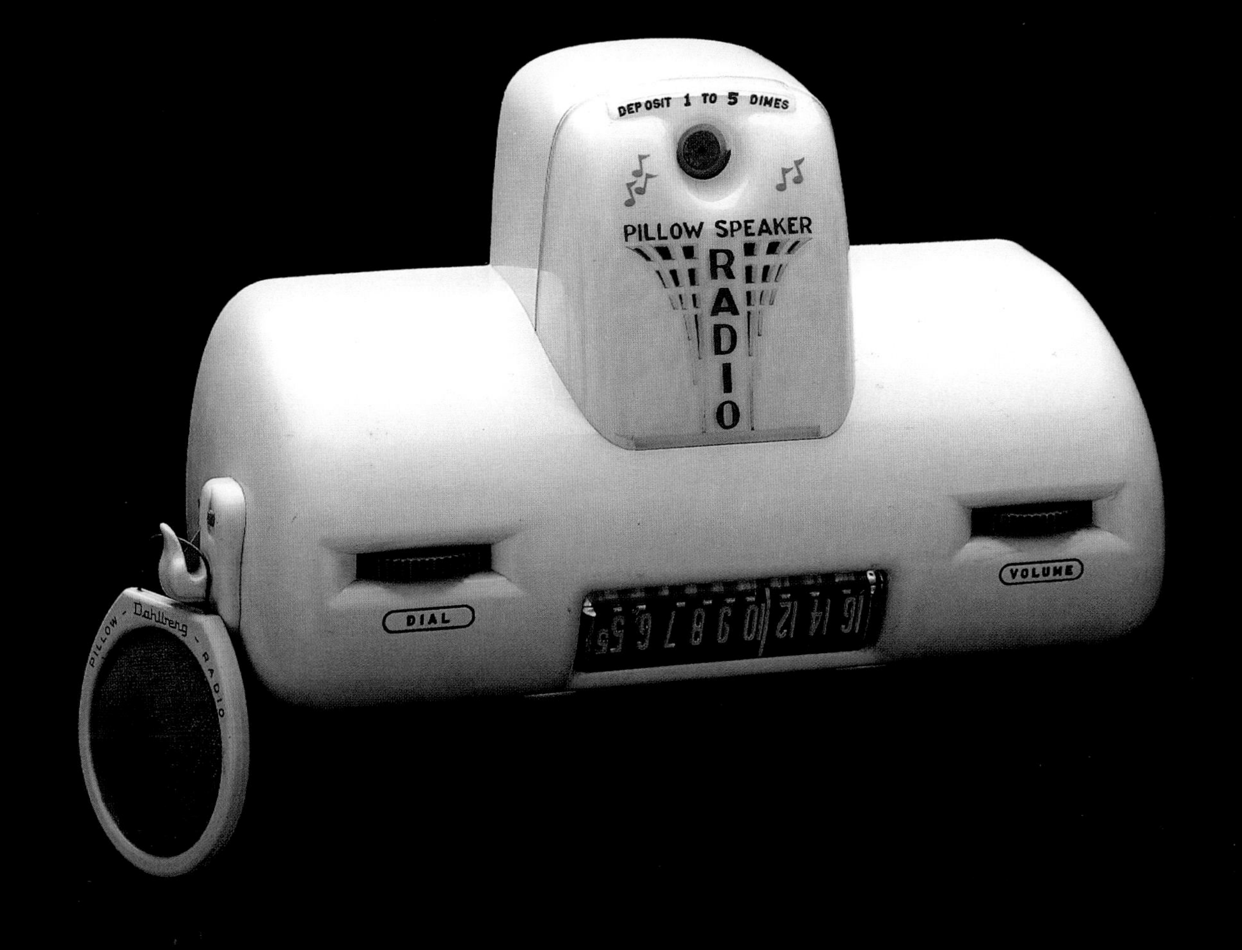

Dahlberg "Pillow Speaker Radio" c. 1955

 "Mike" Radio c. 1957

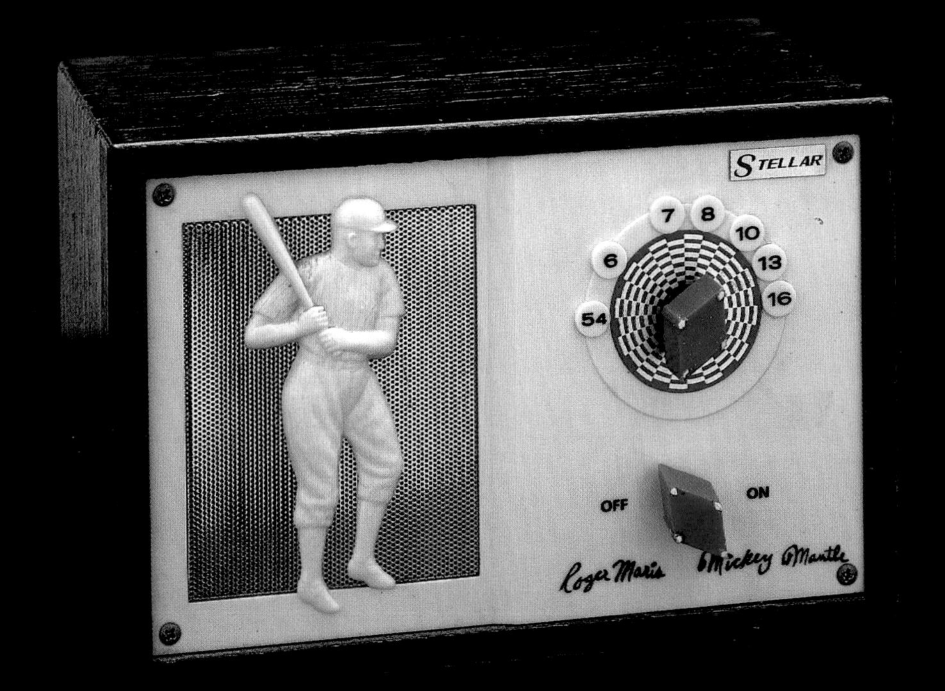

Stellar "Mickey Mantle" c. 1959

DETRON
RADIO TUBE
D
227
DRC

ADVANCE
RADIO
TUBES
ABC
$4.50
484
ADVANCE BATTERY CORP.
TUBE DIVISION
BROOKLYN, NEW YORK
MADE IN U.S.A.

SILVER
DOMINO
RADIO
VACUUM TUBES

RA-1
AMPLIFIER
The
Sonora
A-C
RADIO TUBE
MANUFACTURED ESPECIALLY FOR
SONORA PHONOGRAPH CO.INC. NEW YORK.N.Y.
BY
ARCTURUS RADIO COMPANY—NEWARK.N.J.
PATENTS PENDING

YANKEE
Beats 'em
all-

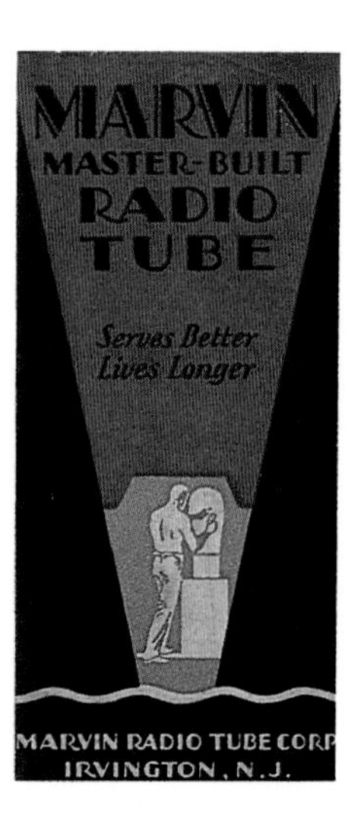
MARVIN
MASTER-BUILT
RADIO
TUBE
Serves Better
Lives Longer
MARVIN RADIO TUBE CORP
IRVINGTON, N.J.

Sky Master c. 1957 (actual size)

NOTES:

Unless otherwise stated, cabinets are manufactured by compression molding in a variety of plastic compounds, mainly Phenol Formaldehyde (Bakelite, Catalin), Urea, and Casein.
The dates refer to the first year of public sale.
The onset of World War II interrupted innovation and production. On their return to post war production in 1946, many companies marketed models originally designed for sale in 1943 and 1944. They also added a new series of designs.
Cosmetic features were sometimes changed, unannounced, altering model numbers of similar sets in a particular range. These vaguaries are often the source of heated debate among the hardened radio collecting fraternity. A changed knob here . . . a revised dial face there — the variety of design between 1932 and 1955 is practically infinite.
The dating and identification of model numbers is based upon original information supplied by manufacturers that has often proved contradictory, however, these discrepancies do not detract from the enjoyment of this golden era in American radio design.

PHOTOGRAPHER'S NOTES:

The radios were photographed with a 4x5 inch view camera, through a 215 mm lens onto 4x5 inch transparency film. Although each set required special lighting for its own unique features, the main light source was a large soft box placed over the subject. An aperture of F/32 was used, and ambient exposures sometimes ranged up to six minutes to capture the faintly lit dials.

Robert Patterson

INDEX:

"A RADIO FOR EVERY ROOM"

Doll's House: Kay Tornborg Collection Radios: Philip Collins Collection

12/13 Emerson

Left: "Mickey Mouse"
Model 411: 1933
Syroco wood
Original condition
Jerry Simpson Collection

Right: "Mickey Mouse"
Model 410: 1933
Wood, metal trim
Refinished
Jerry Simpson Collection

15 Colonial *"New World:" 1933*
Original condition
Courtesy Off the Wall, Melrose Avenue, Los Angeles

16 Stewart Warner: *1933*
Metal
Original condition
Doug Heimstead Collection

17 Unknown *Model C-500: 1934*

Left: Refinished
Jerry Simpson Collection

Center and right:
Original condition
Philip Collins Collection

18 Emerson *Model U5A: 1935*
Original condition
Philip Collins Collection

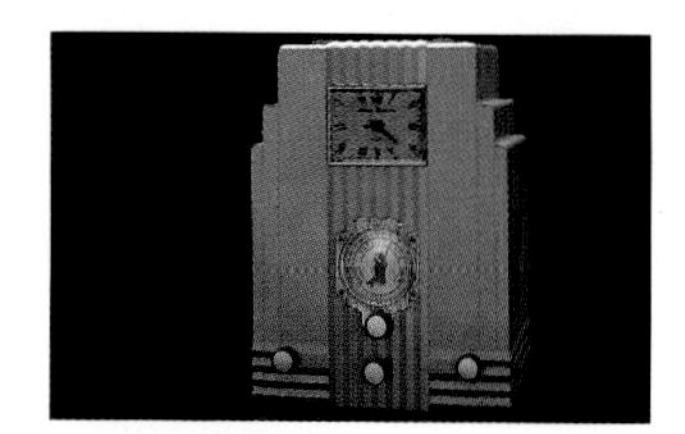

19 Air King: *1935*
Designed by Harold L. Van Doren
and J.G.. Rideout
Refinished
Jerry Simpson Collection

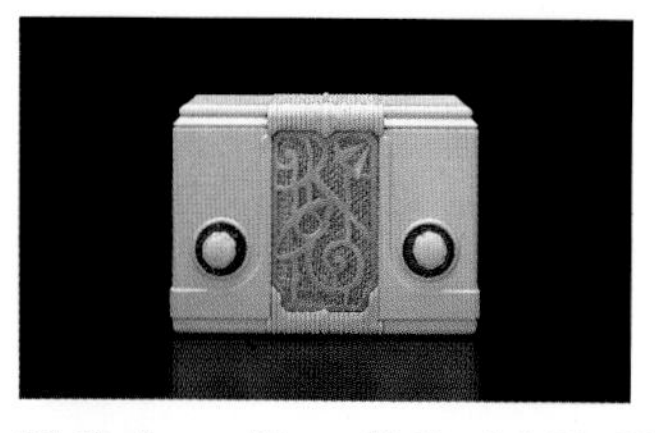

21 Kadette *"Jewel" Model 43: 1935*
Designed by Gardiner Vess
Original condition
Doug Heimstead Collection

24 Unknown: *c.1935*
Mirrored
Original condition
Gary Hough Collection

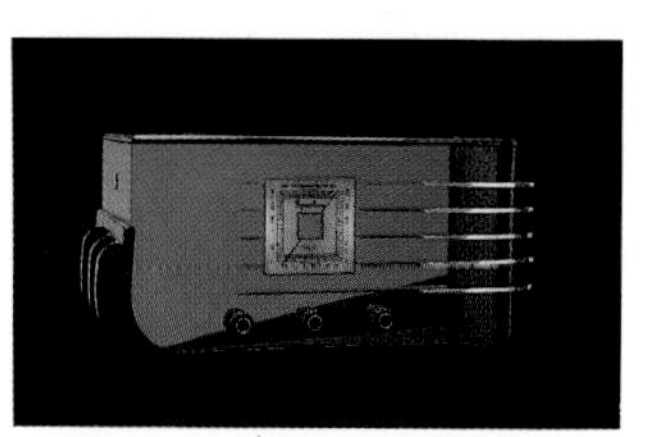

25 Sparton *Model 517: 1936*
Designed by Walter Dorwin Teague
Mirror, chrome, and wood
Refinished
Jerry Simpson Collection

27 Fada *Model 254: 1937*
Original condition
Ed and Irene Ripley Collection

30/31 Emerson
Left: Model 109: 1935
Original condition
Doug Heimstead Collection

Right: Model BA 199: 1938
Original condition
Philip Collins Collection

34 Airite: *1938*
Original condition
Mike Adams Collection

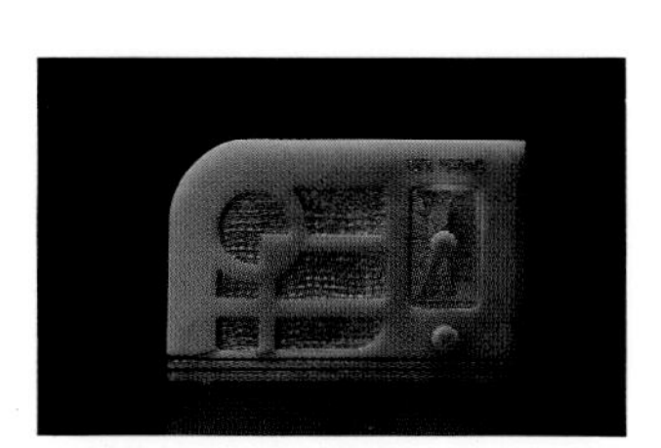

28 Tom Thumb: *1938*
Original condition
Philip Collins Collection

32 Fada: *1938*
Original condition
Philip Collins Collection

35 Majestic *"Charlie McCarthy" Model 1: 1938*
Metal and bakelite
Refinished
Jerry Simpson Collection

29 Emerson *Model AX 235: 1938*
Original condition
Bill Kaplan Collection

33 Detrola *"Peewee": 1938*
Designed by George Walker
Original condition
Doug Heimstead Collection

36 Unknown *c.1938*
Metal, chromed
Refinished
Philip Collins Collection

37 Troy *Model 45-M: 1938*
Mirrored
Original condition
Jerry Simpson Collection

38 Zenith *Model 6D315U: 1938*
Refinished
Philip Collins Collection

39 RCA: *c.1938*
Original condition
Jerry Simpson Collection

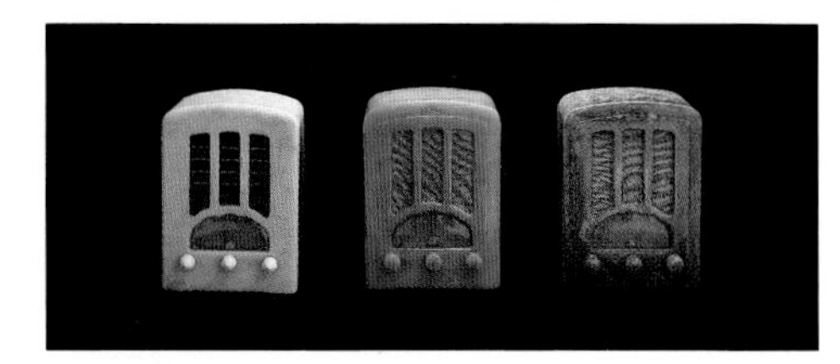

40/41 Emerson
Left: Model BT 245: 1939
Center: Model AU 190: 1938
Right: Model AU 190: 1938
All original condition
Mark Honea Collection

42 Emerson: *c.1939*
Original condition
Philip Collins Collection

43 General Electric *Model H-600: 1939*
Original condition
Philip Collins Collection

45 Fada *Model L 56: 1939*
Original condition
Barry and Ellen Blum Collection

47 Sonora *Model TW 49: 1939*
Original condition
Steve Camargo Collection

48 Belmont *Model 534: 1940*
Refinished
Philip Collins Collection

49 Continental: *c.1940*
Original condition
Ed and Irene Ripley Collection

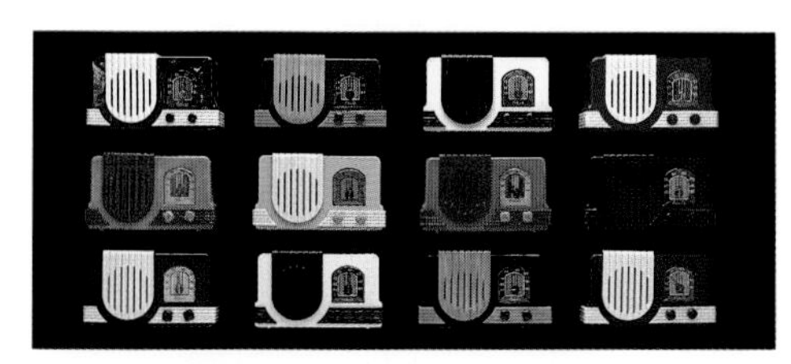

50/51 Addison *Model A2A: c.1940*
Original condition
Mark Honea Collection

53 Emerson *"Patriot"* and *"Aristocrat"*
Model 400: 1940
Designed by Norman Bel Geddes
All original condition
Philip Collins Collection
Bottom row left: Mark Honea Collection

54 Emerson *Model EC301: 1940*
Original condition
Philip Collins Collection

55 *Left:* **Mitchel *"Lumitone" Model 1260: 1940***
Original base
Philip Collins Collection
Right: **Radiolamp Corporation of America:**
c.1940 Refinished
Jerry Simpson Collection

56/57 Addison *Model 5F: c.1940*
All original condition
Mark Honea Collection

58 Garod *"Commander"*
Model 6AU-1: 1941
All original condition
Mark Honea Collection

59 Trophy: *c.1941*
Molded cardboard
Refinished
Jerry Simpson Collection

60 Sonora *"Coronet" Model KM: 1941*
Original condition
Mark Honea Collection

62 General Electric *Model L-622: 1941*
Original condition
William Cawlfield Collection

63 Westinghouse *"Little Jewel"* Model H 124: *1945*
Original condition
Philip Collins Collection

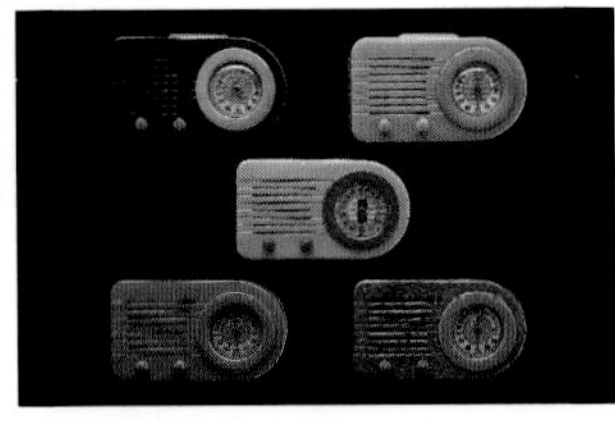

64 Fada *"Streamliner"* Model 1000: 1946
Center row: Model 115: 1941
All original condition
Mark Honea Collection

65 Fada *"Streamliner"* Model 115: 1941
Original condition
Philip Collins Collection

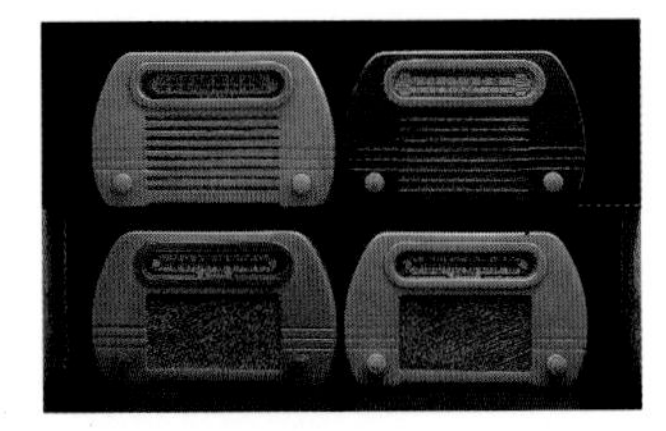

67 Fada *Model 652: 1946*
*Top right:*Model 252
All original condition
Refinished grill cloths
Mark Honea Collection
Top row, left: Philip Collins Collection

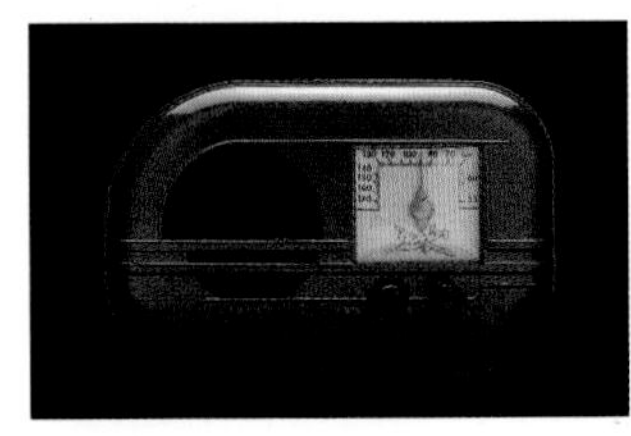

68 Unknown: *c.1946*
Refinished
Philip Collins Collection

69 Belmont *Model 6D 111: 1946*
Refinished
Philip Collins Collection

70 Bendix *Model 115: 1946*
Original condition
Philip Collins Collection

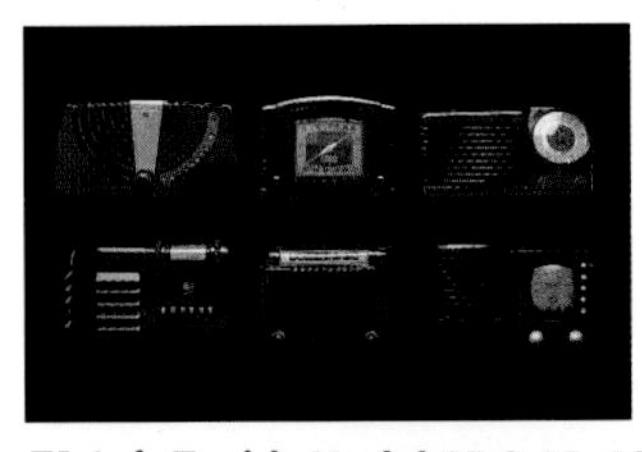

71 *Left:* **Zenith *Model 6DO 15: 1946***
Airline *Model 93 WG 604A: 1946*
Center: ***Trutone Model D 2661: c. 1946***
Bendix *Model 0516A: 1946*
Right: **Olympic *Model 6-501: 1946***
Zenith *Model 5R312: 1938*
All original condition Phillip Collins Collection

72 Stewart Warner *Model 62T36: 1946*
Original condition
Mark Honea Collection

73 Majestic *"Melody Cruiser" Model 921: c.1946*
Wood and chrome
Refinished
Clyde Plott Collection

74 DeWald *Model A502: 1946*
Original condition
Courtesy Harvey's; Melrose Avenue, Los Angeles

75 Airline: *c.1946*
Left: 64BR-1501A 64BR-1501A 64BR-1501A
Center: 84BR-1502B 4BR-511A 84BR-1502B
Right: 4BR-511A 84BR-1502S 4BR-511A
All models refinished
Philip Collins Collection

76 Crosley *"Duette" Model 56 TD: 1946*
Refinished
Philip Collins Collection

77 Coronado *Model 43-8190: 1947*
Original condition
Mark Honea Collection

78 Stewart Warner *"Air Pal" Model A51T3: 1947*
Refinished grill cloth
Philip Collins Collection

79 Sentinel *Model L-284: 1947*
Original condition
Mark Honea Collection

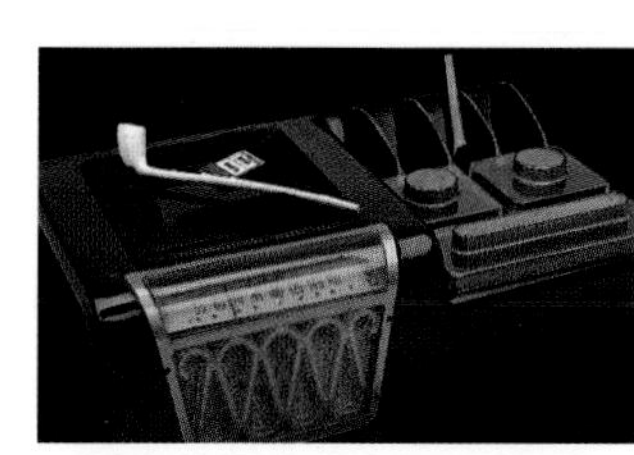

80/81 Porto Products *"Smokerette": 1947*
Designed by Barnes & Reinecke
Original condition
Philip Collins Collection

83 Belmont *Model 6D120: 1947*
Refinished
Philip Collins Collection

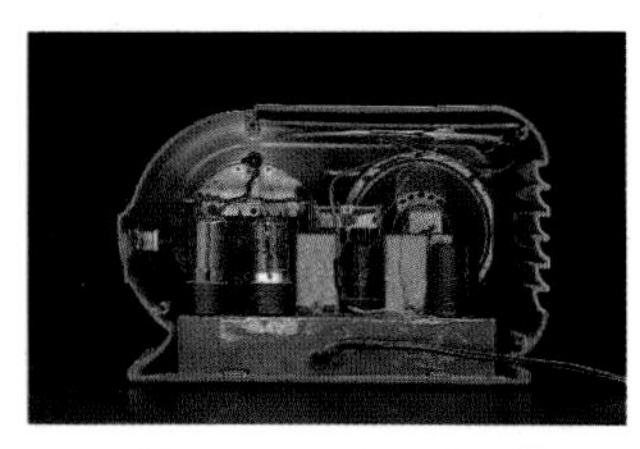

84 Behind the Painted Smile

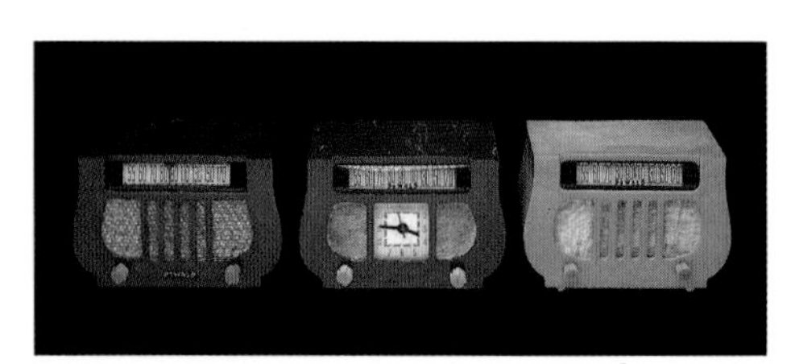

86/87 DeWald
Left: Model A-501: 1941. Philip Collins Collection
Center: Model B-403: 1948. Mark Honea Collection
Right: Model B-501 UL: 1941. Mark Honea Collection
All in original condition

89 Point of Purchase Displays, Inc.
"Coca-Cola Cooler"
Model 5A 410A: 1949
Refinished
Jerry Simpson Collection

91 Arvin *"Hopalong Cassidy" Model 441-T: 1950*
Original condition
Philip Collins Collection

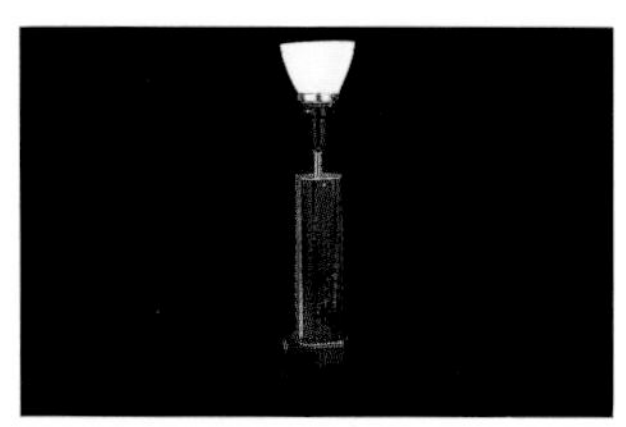

92 Unknown: *c.1950*
Brass and metal
Refinished
Jerry Simpson Collection

93 Arvin *Model 440-T: 1950*
Chromed
Refinished metal
Philip Collins Collection

94 Arvin *Model 541 TL: 1950*
Original condition
Philip Collins Collection

95 Majestic *Model 5 LA 5: 1951*
Refinished
Philip Collins Collection

96 Silvertone *Model 4:233: 1951*
Refinished
Jerry Simpson Collection

97 Crosley
Left: Model D10TN: 1951
Center: Model 11 100U: 1951
Right: Model 11 102U: 1951
All in original condition
Barry and Ellen Blum Collection

98 Airline *"Rudolph:" 1951*
Original condition
Ed and Irene Ripley Collection

99 Airline *"Lone Ranger" Model 05GCB-1541: 1951*
Original condition
Ed and Irene Ripley Collection

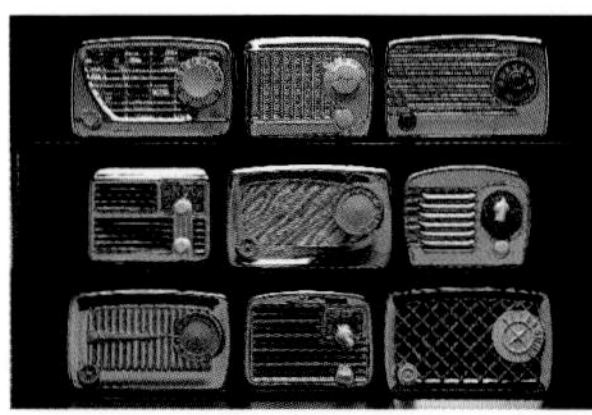

100 Arvin and Silvertone *Left*: Arvin Model 842J: 1947
Arvin Model 444: 1946 Arvin 840T: 1954
Center: Arvin Model 242T: 1948 Arvin: c.1955
Silvertone Model 6002: 1946 *Right*: Arvin Model 422A
Silvertone: c.1949 Silvertone Model 1: 1950
Refinished metal and chrome Philip Collins Collection

101 Dahlberg *"Pillow Speaker Radio" Model 430-D1: c.1955*
Note the inverted dial for the convenience
of the reclining listener
Original condition
Courtesy Harvey's, Melrose Avenue, Los Angeles

102 "Mike" Radio: *c.1957*
Original condition
Bob Breed Collection

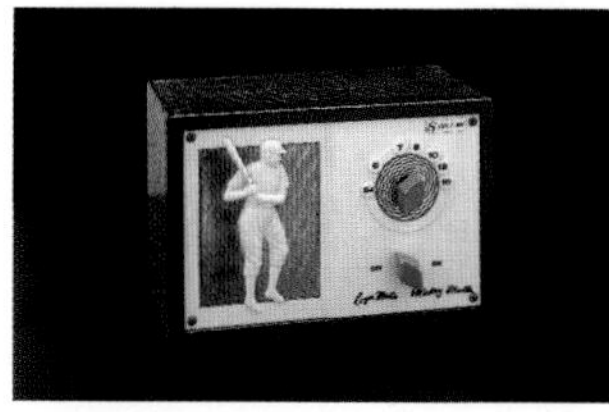

103 Stellar *"Mickey Mantle:" c.1959*
Japanese
Wood cabinet
Original condition
Philip Collins Collection

105 Sky Master *Model PR 530: c.1957*
Original condition
One of the last models to utilize 'peanut' tubes
Philip Collins Collection

COLLECTORS:

Grateful thanks are due to the following collectors:

Mike Adams
(714) 779-7907
Collecting wood, console and plastics
Complete restoration of wood radios

Barry and Ellen Blum
(213) 274-6662
Collecting all plastics and novelty

Charles Bradley
(612) 888-7437
Collecting radio memorabilia

Bob Breed
(619) 274-0712
Collecting novelty and transistor novelty

Steve Camargo
3730 1st. Avenue #7
San Diego, Ca. 92103
Collecting plastics

William Cawlfield
(818) 368-9060
Collecting plastics and novelty
Restoration of all sets

Philip Collins
(213) 479-0167
Collecting Catalin, bakelite, mirrored, metal and novelty

Doug Heimstead
(612) 571-1387
Collecting mirrored, plastics and televisions
Restoration and repair of radios and televisions

Mark Honea
(816) 891-2441
Collecting catalin, mirrored and novelty

Gary Hough
(714) 835-5765
Collecting vintage TV's, mirrored and catalin radios

Bill Kaplan
(213) 379-3399
Collecting wood console and table
Complete restoration and repair

Joe Knight
(213) 831-5556
Collecting anciliary radio artefacts and memorabilia

Clyde Plott
(805) 255-4600
Collecting wood table and console

Ed and Irene Ripley
(612) 777-6791
Collecting plastics, wood, novelty and mirrored

Jerry Simpson
(805) 251-7829
Collecting wood, novelty, plastics and mirrored
Complete restoration of all sets

BIBLIOGRAPHY:

Radio Retailing Magazine: 1937-39
Radio & Television Retailing Magazine: 1939-41
Radio Guide Magazine: 1939
Volksempfanger by Dieter Holtschmidt: 1981
The Cat's Whisker by Jonathan Hill, Oresko Books Ltd.: 1978
Dime-Store Dream Parade by Robert Heide and John Gilman, E.P. Dutton: 1979
Gli Anni di Plastica by Pasquale Alferj and Franscesca Cernia, Electa: 1983
Art Plastic by Andrea DiNoto, Abbeville: 1984
Plastics by Sylvia Katz, Thames & Hudson: 1984
Small Radio, Emerson Radio & Phonograph Corp.: 1943
Radio for the Millions, Popular Science Publishing Co.: 1945
Industrial Design by John Heskett, Thames & Hudson: 1980
Antique Radios by David and Betty Johnson, Wallace Homestead: 1983
Encyclopedia of Collectibles, Time Life Books Inc.: 1980
A Flick of the Switch by Morgan E. McMahon, Vintage Radio: 1975
The Radio Collectors Directory by Robert Grinder and George H. Fathauer, Ironwood Press: 1986
General Plastics by Raymond Cherry, McKnight & McKnight: 1941
The Story of Plastic Molding, Chicago Molded Products Corp.: 1940
Plastics Catalog, Plastic Catalog Corp.: 1943
The Encyclopedia of Antique Radio by J.W.F. Puett, Puett Electronics: 1979 and 1980
Photo Facts, Howard Sams & Co.: 1946-51

ACKNOWLEDGMENTS:

For their various courtesies and generous cooperation, thanks are due to:

Bob Breed
Richard Compton
Doug Heimstead
Bevis Hillier
Mark Honea
Morgan McMahon
Michael McCormick
Oscar Melton
Richard Nitz
Robert Patterson
Larry Pippick
Ed and Irene Ripley
Arnold Schwartzman
Edward Shelton
Jerry Simpson
Kay Tornborg
Baron Wolman
Amy Yutani

PERMISSIONS:

Emerson "Patriot" and "Raymond Loewy" advertisements: courtesy Emerson Radio Corp.
Hopalong Cassidy Instruction Leaflet: by kind permission of Arvin Industries Inc.
Coca-Cola advertisement: courtesy of the Archives. The Coca-Cola Company.
Belmont Radio Schematic used by the courtesy of the publisher, Howard W. Sams & Co.
'Raised On Radio' logo: courtesy Herbie Herbert Management Inc.
Tube box motifs: courtesy Joe Knight Collection.
Radio ephemera: courtesy Charles Bradley Collection.
The Daily News, October 31, 1938 courtesy The Daily News.

CROSSWORD SOLUTION

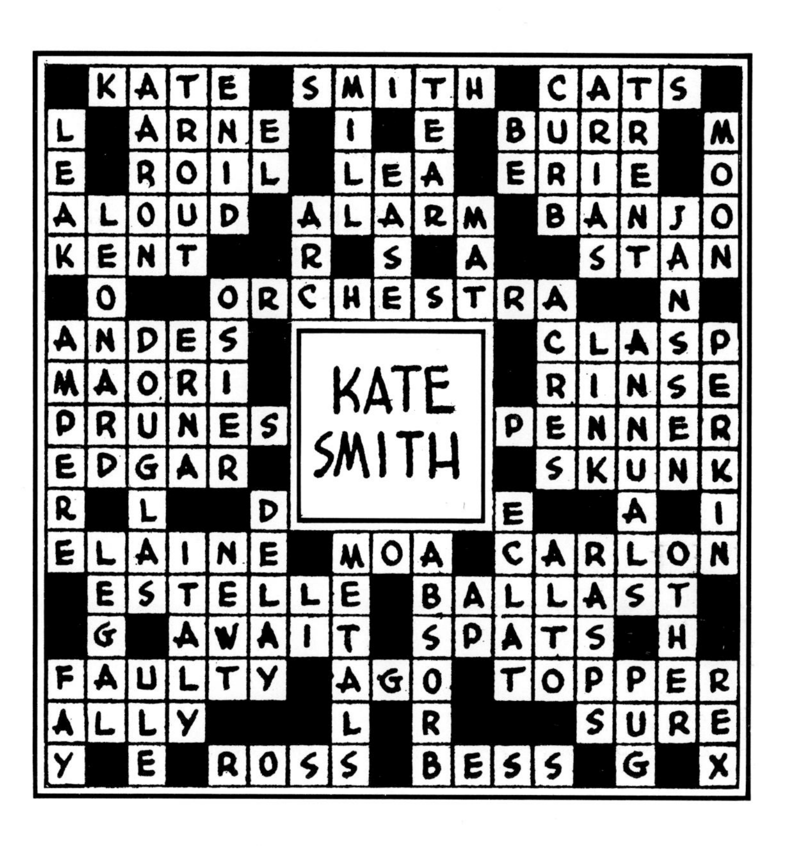